Screen Shots

Multimedia computing

Multimedia computing

Chouka

CASSELL&CO

First published, revised and adapted in the United Kingdom in 2000 by Hachette UK

© English Translation Hachette UK 2000
© Hachette Livre: Marabout Informatique 1999

English translation by Prose Unlimited and Dominique Laloux
Concept and editorial direction: Ghéorghïi Vladimirovitch Grigorieff
Additional research and editorial assistance: Simon Woolf, Mac Duff, Paul Ward, David Penfold, Jane Eady, Johan Rinchard and John Cardinal.

A CIP catalogue for this book is available from the British Library

Trademarks/Registered Trademarks

Computer hardware and software brand names mentioned in this book are protected by their respective trademarks and acknowledged. Every effort has been made to make this book as complete and accurate as possible, but the publisher and author cannot accept any responsibility for any loss or inconvenience sustained by any reader as a result of this book's information or advice.

ISBN 1 84202 043 9

Designed by Graph'M
Layout by Dimitri Culot
Typeset in Humanist 521
Printed and bound by Graficas Estella, Spain

Hachette UK
Cassell & Co
The Orion Publishing Group
Wellington House
London
WC2R 0BB

Web site: www.marabout.com/Cassell

Contents

How Screen Shots works

Welcome to this visual guide. It explains how to carry out some one hundred or so operations, ranging from the simple to the more complex, in a clear and methodical manner. This book is divided into thematic chapters, which are in turn divided into sections. Each section deals with a separate topic and explains its many facets and uses, as well as detailing all related commands.

The orange 'Checklist' bookmarks that appear throughout the book contain lists of the procedures you must follow in order to complete a given task succesfully. The accompanying screen shots have arrows pointing to certain parts of the screen. When the points in the checklists are numbered, they correspond directly with these numbered green arrows. When the points in the bookmarks bear letters they do not relate directly to the arrows, but simply provide additional useful information. When the arrows pointing to the screen are orange they give information on a particular feature, whilst the red arrows alert you of a possible danger, such as a button to avoid pressing at all costs!

In addition to illustrations of relevant screen shots as they should appear if instructions have been followed correctly, the Screen Shots series also features 'Tips' boxes and 'light-bulb' features that will help you get the most from you computer. The 'Tips' boxes give handy time-saving hints, while the light-bulb features provide additional information by presenting an associated command, option or particular type of use for the command. Finally, to reassure you that you are on the right path, flow charts summarising the screen shots through which you have just worked, appear at intervals throughout the book.

Happy reading...

How to use this book

Menu/Command

← This line displays the location of the command that is needed to carry out the procedure (*File/Open* in the case of opening files, for example). To make matters easier, the following convention is used: the first part (in this case *'File'*) refers to the drop down menu and the second part (in this case *'Open'*) refers to the command you must select.

The introductory text to each section explains its contents. It begins by answering a few questions: What is the main command illustrated in the section used for? Can it be combined with others? Is there a 'right' and a 'wrong' way to use this command?

You will then find definitions when new elements appear (the cells in the sections on tables, compression in the section on WinZip, etc.).

You will also find tips and hints displayed throughout in the style shown on this page.

HOW TO

The 'How To' box can assume several forms. It is usually combined with a screen snapshot. This illustration shows an image enhanced using photo-editing software, an example of the results if the command is carried out properly. The box then displays a 'how to' procedure, like a 'recipe', with the settings selected in the main windows, as presented in detail in the pages which follow.

TIP

This purple circle contains a tip, recommendation or warning specific to the current section.

Close a file

Location of the command opening the window presented on this page.

File/Close

Icon that automatically opens the window presented on this page when you click on it with the left button of the mouse.

A green arrow:
A step of the procedure, identified by its number (see checklist). The arrow indicates the place to click.

❶ Click the command.

❷ Click to close the document.

An orange arrow:
A tip, a hint, a box you can click without fear...

Click to go back to the active window without changing anything.

Warning: if you click here you will lose your last changes.

A red arrow:
Warning: danger!

[Ctrl] + [W]

Shortcut keys: **This is a combination of keys, the effect of which is equivalent clicking a command in the menu: press these two or three keys simultaneously to display the window presented on the page.**

A tip, hint or more detailed explanation

Checklist

❶ Click *File/Close.*

❷ Click *Yes* if you wish to save the file.
The program closes the current file but remains active.

This checklist goes step-by-step over the procedure to follow in order to carry out the task successfully. Each step is identified by a number. The numbers of the checklist correspond to the numbers of the arrows. Information contained in the checklist is generally more complete than that which accompanies the arrows.

Program installation sequence...

Some commands activate a series of installation dialogue boxes.
Some dialogue boxes lead to four or five other boxes of lesser
importance...

This checklist is used
to explain important
dialogue boxes that
appear when you attempt
to install.

It contains a brief
description or explanation.
If it is red, be warned
and retrace your steps
because it is informing you
that you clicked in the
wrong place. If it is orange
you run no risk, but the
window is not vital.

Windows displays a
conclusion box.
Click *Details* to display the
devices detected. Click
Finish for Windows to install the drivers. If no device
was detected, restart the
installation and proceed
manually.

Before you install the
drivers, Windows will
display a last confirmation
screen with the
characteristics of the
device.

Click to return to the
control panel without
installing.

This box usually
contains addi-
tional information
concerning the
underlying theory.

It also goes into
greater depth
to explain how
the computer
performs a given
function and what
difficulties you
might experience
with a certain
task.

If appropriate, we refer you to
a related page.

The button to click to
access the next dialog box
is indicated.

The arrows are directed
from the outgoing box to
the incoming box.

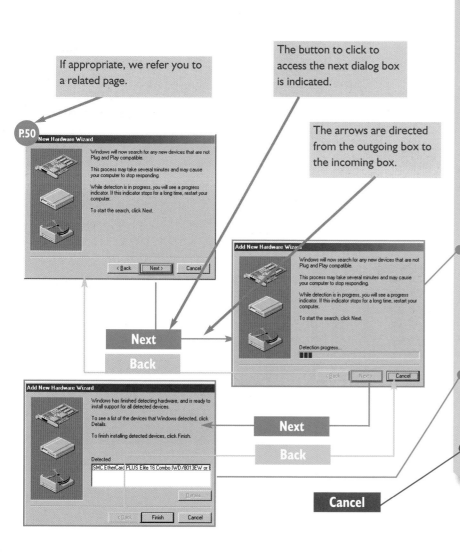

Next

Back

Next

Back

Cancel

Examples

These pages present:

A summary of the possibilities offered by the headings of a window; or

A summary of the possibilities concerning a specific topic (e.g. there are many ways to create a chart in MS-Word). In this case, the commands and settings used are indicated; or

A step-by-step description of a rather complex procedure to carry out a small project successfully.

Step 1

Insert an audio CD in the CD-ROM drive. This automatically calls the CD player. The next section of this book covers the Audio CD Player.

Step 2
Open the Sound Recorder and the Recording Control (*Edit/Audio Properties*). All the tools are ready to start the recording.

Stacked bar charts

Used to compare expenses in relation to time (total expenses and distribution).

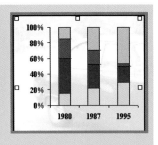

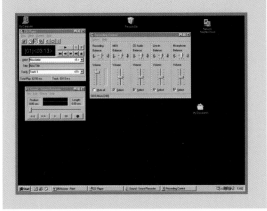

INTRODUCTION

Introduction

Multimedia. The very word evokes the pooling of various types of information to create a graphics and sound studio in your own home. While in the past this might have been just a fantasy, with the advent of increasingly powerful hardware and superior storage mediums such as Zip, CD's and Syquest, it is now very much a reality. Virtually every home computing system on the market today boasts an array of multimedia equipment, from video and soundcards to CD-ROMs and CD recorders. With your multimedia PC, you will be able to listen to the sound effect of the latest games, listen to an audio CD inserted in the CD-ROM drive, customise your computer by recording sounds and programming them to play back every time you boot up and much much more.

If you want your computer to do even more, all you have to do is install new programs such as Adobe Photoshop, Paint Shop Pro or Premiere, or download a piece of software from the Internet such as MP3. You can then start the 'multimedia' processing of files: retouching holiday photographs, mixing sounds 'grabbed' from a CD or running together two video clips while defining a background effect for the transition from one to the other. While the above applications can be used to create professional results, it does not take a computer whiz to use them – in fact, all you need is this book.

As for the future, there are no boundaries. While purists might argue that our computers cannot be truly multimedia until they engage all our senses, technology is advancing so rapidly, even this argument will soon be redundant. This year, a British company has begun work on an 'odorama' system that will allow you to literally smell what you see on screen, through the use of scent capsules controlled by your computer. Soon you will be able to catch a whiff of the breath of Quake monsters, or perhaps smell a tarte tatin featured on a CD-ROM devoted to French cuisine. This is science fiction no longer, because in information technology, no idea goes to waste.

But for the time being, we invite you to surprise the people around you by putting the programs already installed on your PC to good use, and to go even further with your creativity and imagination thanks to a few additional programs.

Have fun!

Chapter 1

General

Introducing the multimedia computer

A multimedia computer is an ordinary computer with some built-in features that can read and manage sound and image data. All multimedia computers are fitted with a sound card for reading, reproducing and recording sound files. They also contain a **CD-ROM** drive and a battery of small, rather basic but reliable and useful programs for enjoying the contents of **CD-ROMs** (images, video clips, narrative text, sounds, etc.). Any computer can in fact be turned into a 'multimedia' machine by installing a sound card, a **CD-ROM** drive and the right programs. And that is not all. Depending on your budget, you can easily turn a multimedia **PC** into a multimedia studio (with the **PC** as its core). All you have to do is add a scanner, a photographic quality colour inkjet printer, a digital photo device, a microphone, a modem to access the Internet, a synthesiser or a camcorder and a video acquisition card. If you install software capable of managing the data transmitted by these devices, and if the characteristics of the machine make it possible, you will find yourself at the controls of a small, semi-professional studio. Of course, depending on areas of specialisation (sound engineer, photographer, etc.), professionals, all of whom use computers, have access to more powerful or more sophisticated programs.

TIP

You will choose what programs to install depending on your areas of interest (photography, video production, sound mixing, etc.). Thus, a photographer will have to have a digital camera and a flatbed scanner to transfer the images to the computer, an image retouching program (Adobe Photoshop, Paint Shop Pro or a program delivered with the camera) and a photo quality colour printer to output the work.

The photographer's studio

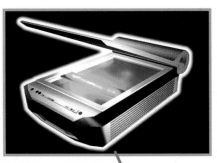

Digital camera
A conventional camera from the outside, but here the film has been replaced by a CCD sensor (a small device, the size of a 24x36 negative, composed of thousands of photosensitive cells that record the intensity and the colours of light). The camera is equipped with a cable which can be connected to the PC to download the photographs.

Scanner
A device for digitising images and text from paper. A scanner works like a photocopier, with the difference that, instead of making a copy of the original on paper, it produces a digital copy.

Storage medium
Must be able to store and carry files up to 50 Mb in size (a high resolution photo can be easily this size).

Colour printer
Colour inkjet printer to keep down costs. Must be capable of photographic quality printing on photographic-quality paper.

A small image retouching studio will consist, as we said on the previous page, of a digital camera (the image is digitised when the shot is taken) or a scanner (the photograph is developed in a conventional manner and then transformed into digital data via the scanner), an image retouching program and a photographic quality colour printer or a suitable storage medium.

Image retouching programs are divided into two categories: 'hobby' and 'semi-professional.' The first are usually packaged with digital cameras and are open to all: easy to use, they enable you to achieve very nice tricks with three clicks of the mouse. The second, such as Adobe Photoshop or Paint Shop Pro, are far more powerful and feature many functions, built-in filters, etc. The snag is that learning to use them takes time: the procedures are often long and relatively complex, even though a great deal of progress has been made through the various versions to simplify the various procedures. Adobe Photoshop remains the standard among professional photographers.

Sound input devices remain highly complementary. They include, first, the CD-ROM drive, used to extract music or sound tracks from an audio CD. Then there is the microphone (good quality is imperative) that the amateur sound engineer will use to record voices, background sounds, sound effects, etc. Finally, composers will need a synthesiser or, better still, a simple master keyboard (a keyboard identical to that of a synthesiser but less expensive, because it has neither memory nor sound database, both of which are relatively unimportant as the components of the PC contain all the necessary features). To process the sound, you will need to buy a good quality sound card, at the very least a SoundBlaster 64 PnP (for Plug and Play). This card contains a sound mixer, a recording table, a sound database, MIDI editor, etc. It provides the backbone of the 'recording studio'.

A pair of good quality speakers is essential for the sound output or reproduction.

If you have the money, you might consider buying a CD recorder. Though not cheap, they are gradually falling in price, and allow you to record your own music on compact disc. This can then be played back on any Hi-Fi system.

The sound studio

Microphone
Used to record your own sounds.

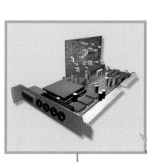

Master keyboard or synthesiser
For composing pieces and sending them to the PC for processing.

Sound card
Set in the PC case, the sound card is at the centre of sound recording, reproduction, and processing.

CD recorder
Also a CD-ROM drive, the CD recorder is used to record sound (or images, video clips, etc.). CDs intended for such use are known as CD-R ('Recordable') or CD-RW ('Re-writable').

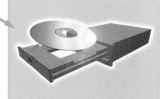

Speakers
Same as the speakers of a Hi-Fi system; they must be able to reproduce good quality sound without hissing or distortion.

Storage medium
Must be able to store and carry files up to 50 Mb.

The video studio

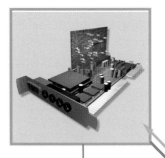

Video capture card
Set in the case of the PC, the video capture card is used to transfer images from an external medium to the computer.

Camcorder
The hand-held camera par excellence for putting the enduring memories of dream holidays on film. Analogue or digital.

Video recorder
The current standard for recording and viewing films.

DVD (Digital Versatile Disk)
A high quality digital video format also being used for games. Will gradually VCRs.

A camcorder or video cassette recorder will send images and sound to the PC through a connection cable. But you can also extract video files from other media, such as CD-ROM, DVD-ROM, etc.

At the computer level, a video card is quite welcome. This card will convert an analogue ('standard') image into a digital image if the input device (see below) is a standard VCR or camcorder, or it will copy a digital image from a digital camcorder.

Inside the computer, editing software like Adobe Premiere provides users with all the necessary editing tools.

You will also need a tool to save the image, either on a computerised medium such as a large capacity storage diskette – a Zip drive (100 Mb per cartridge), a Jazz (1000 Mb or 1 Gb per cartridge), or a CD-R (640 Mb) – or on an analogue medium. If you have a video conversion card, you can also record the film to a small format video tape (VHS-C, 8 mm…).

'Digitalise', 'digitise', 'scan': three synonyms that mean convert an image into (digital) data. The basic principle of digitisation, whether done by a scanner or video capture card, is based on the conversion of analogue signals into digital signals. An image recorded on tape, or the grooves on a 33 vinyl disc turned into electric pulses for speakers are two examples of an analogue signal. A digital signal is a binary signal. All information is reduced to a series of 0s and 1s (text, colour, sound frequency, etc.). The computer is really an immense manager of electric micro-currents: '1', the current passes; '0' the current does not pass, as in switches (see also page 60).

File management basics

There is nothing more frustrating than not being able to find a file you created the night before! In order to store and supply all the information it gobbles up, a hard disk must be organised flawlessly. Like all 'filing cabinets', it houses sub-divisions, which are in turn divided into smaller elements. In an office, the filing cabinets can be divided into sections holding files with sub-divisions. The same principle applies in information technology: the disk is organised into several directories (or folders). Each directory may contain sub-directories that contain files. A file is the smallest filing unit, which usually takes the form of a presentation, a drawing, a photograph or a small program. The collection of files and directories – a veritable electronic spider's web – is called a tree structure.

HOW TO

Windows uses a program called Explorer to show the structure of the drives and folders on the PC. It displays, on the left, the tree structure of the computer drives. On the right are the files stored in the directory selected in the left pane. In our example, the hard disk (**c:**) is divided into directories (Derive, Larousse, My Documents, etc.). My Documents, for example, is subdivided into sub-directories (mp3, ideas, etc.). The selected (open) sub-directory (mp3) contains the files displayed in the right pane of the screen.

TIP

In information technology, we often speak of an access path. This is a symbolic representation of the path to follow through the directories in order to reach a file. Let us imagine a file called Letter.doc, in the sub-directory Mail, itself belonging to the directory My documents, located, as it should be, on the hard disk(c:). The access path for this file would be: c:\My Documents\ Mail \ Letter.doc. The backslash (\) acts as a separator.

Description of the main components of Explorer

Start / Windows Explorer

Title bar
Indicates the name of the selected folder.

Menu bar
Contains all the Explorer commands.

Toolbar
Features illustrated buttons that work as shortcuts for commands.

Window management buttons
To minimise, maximise and close a window.

Left pane
Displays the PC's drives and folders and shows which directory is selected. A plus (+) to the left indicates that the directory contains sub-directories that are not shown.

The Explorer window in Windows 98 has changed from that of the Windows 95 Explorer: it is now closer to the navigation window found in Microsoft's Internet Explorer.

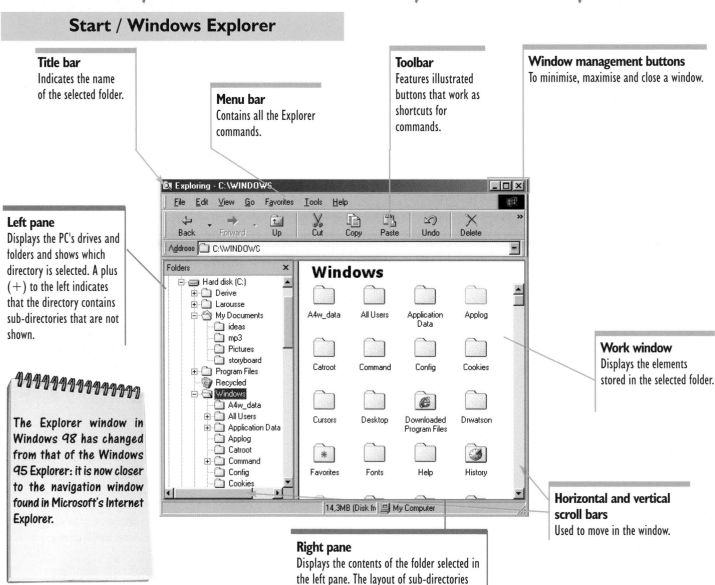

Work window
Displays the elements stored in the selected folder.

Horizontal and vertical scroll bars
Used to move in the window.

Right pane
Displays the contents of the folder selected in the left pane. The layout of sub-directories and files can be changed to view file sizes, locations, etc.

Checklist

1. Double-click the *My Computer* icon, on the desktop. Then click the *CD-ROM drive* (usually (d: or e:)). Windows opens an exploration window. Do the same for the hard disk (usually (c:)) by double-clicking its icon. A second exploration window is opened, which displays the contents of the hard disk.

2. Arrange the two windows so that they are easily accessible. Click to select the file to be copied in the CD-ROM window.

3. Keep the left button of the mouse pressed (with the pointer on the selected file) and drag the file to the hard disk window. All you have to do is move the mouse on the desktop.

4. A ghost file follows the movement of your wrist. Just stop on the folder that is to host the file.

5. The folder into which the file will be copied if you release the mouse button is displayed in reverse video (it appears 'selected'). Release the button to 'drop' the file in it.

Copy a file (from a CD-ROM to a hard disk)

Contextual menu/Copy

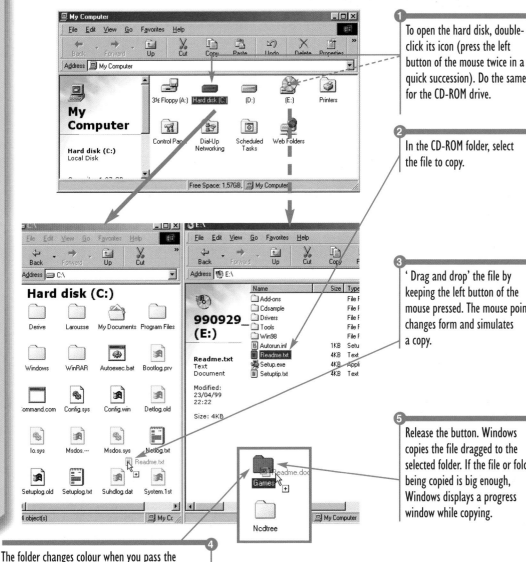

1. To open the hard disk, double-click its icon (press the left button of the mouse twice in a quick succession). Do the same for the CD-ROM drive.

2. In the CD-ROM folder, select the file to copy.

3. 'Drag and drop' the file by keeping the left button of the mouse pressed. The mouse pointer changes form and simulates a copy.

5. Release the button. Windows copies the file dragged to the selected folder. If the file or folder being copied is big enough, Windows displays a progress window while copying.

4. The folder changes colour when you pass the mouse pointer over it. It is 'selected.'

Create a new folder

File/New/Folder

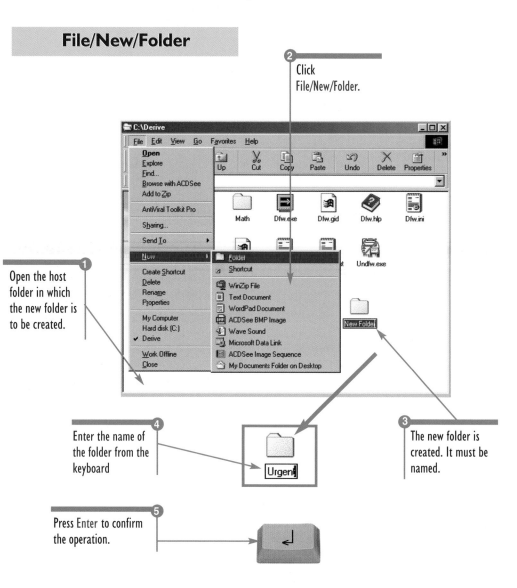

Click
File/New/Folder.

Open the host
folder in which
the new folder is
to be created.

Enter the name of
the folder from the
keyboard

The new folder is
created. It must be
named.

Press Enter to confirm
the operation.

Urgent

Different views for a folder

The View menu of the Explorer offers four different view options: Large Icons, Small Icons, List and Details. These options do not change the contents of the folders. They simply display the contents in different ways. To view a maximum of information in the selected folder, select Details (which displays the size, the type and the date the files were modified). To list the contents of a very large folder, select List. However, if you have a lot of space and like to see things large, select Large Icons...

Large Icons
The main information concerning the selected object is displayed on the left side of the window. Notice the contents of the view menu, presented on this screen snapshot.

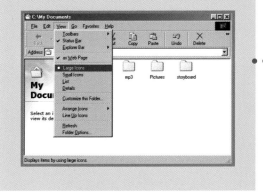

Small Icons

Here, once again, the information concerning the selected object is displayed on the left of the window. Notice how little space the information takes up here compared with the Large Icons view.

Details

Each line details information concerning the file to which it pertains. You can stretch the window horizontally in order to display all the information.

File/Folder viewing examples

In Windows 98, there are three ways to view Files/Folders: Web style, Classic Style or Custom (style). In Web style, the items are underlined in black. When the mouse pointer moves over an object, the object is automatically selected and the pointer turns into a pointed finger. Just click once to open the object. This style may require a little time to get used to, but Internet users will get the hang of it immediately. In Classic style, you will find the Windows 95 windows. Here, you must click twice to open an object. Finally, the Custom (style), based on the settings you choose, enables you to create your own style by selecting one option or another depending on the topic (view folders, active desktop, click, etc.).

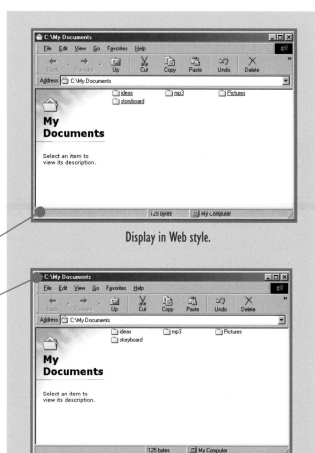

Display in Web style.

Display in Classic style.

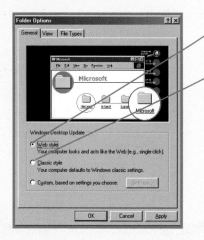

Tick the option you want.

Introducing the peripherals

In information technology, we draw a distinction between the **PC** (the computer and its internal components, such as the expansion cards) and the peripherals, which are external devices that can be connected to the computer (keyboard, mouse, scanner, printer, etc.).

Among the peripherals, we draw a distinction between input devices, used to transfer data to the computer and output devices, which transfer data outside the computer. Input devices include the mouse, for example, which transfers movements and clicks from the user to the programs and the scanner which digitises an image and transfers it to the computer. Output devices include printers, which put on paper text from a word-processing program, and speakers, which produce sound from audio files.

For their part, the storage peripherals play a unique role: they store data and, in some cases, help to transport it. The diskette is still the peripheral most commonly used for storing data, in spite of its limited capacity. The size of documents is growing steadily, and new storage media have been developed. Zip cartridges, for example, can store up to 250 Mb of data, the equivalent of 170 standard (1.44 Mb) diskettes.

The computer may be faced with conflicts between peripherals attempting to use the resources: processing priority (or 'interrupt'), memory range, etc. In the event of conflict, the symptoms are numerous and unforeseeable, ranging from an imperceptible slow-down of the **CD-ROM** drive to the complete refusal to restart or a system error.

Connecting the peripherals

Keyboard connector (on the keyboard port).

Mouse (on mouse port).

Digital camera connector.

Printer connector (on the parallel port).

Monitor (on video card).

Telephone set connector (on the modem).

Speakers and microphone (on the sound card).

Scanner connector (on the parallel port or a SCSI port).

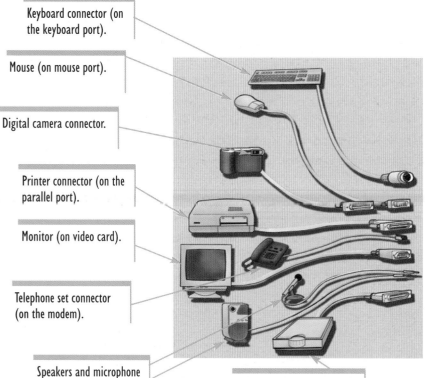

All peripherals are connected to the computer by means of a specific connection cable. Some peripherals are connected directly to the standard ports of the PC. This is the case of the printer (which is connected to the parallel port), the keyboard (keyboard port), the mouse (mouse port) and internal components. Other peripherals are connected to various expansion cards you have installed in the computer (sound card, video capture card, etc.). Each peripheral has a cable with connectors adapted to the transmition of video images, stereo sound, or simpler signals, as in the case of the mouse.
This means that each peripheral is plugged into a particular socket, usually at the back of the computer.

Bear in mind that the appearance of Universal Serial Bus (or USB) ports will change this profusion of electrical wires somewhat. The USB port, which appeared in 1997, and is now widely available on new PCs, is capable of managing by itself 127 connected devices. USB ports not only simplify the connection of peripherals, but they also increase the data flow rates, thus speeding up multimedia tasks.

Expansion cards

Most peripherals are connected to expansion cards installed inside the **PC**. An expansion card is a green card teeming with integrated circuits, condensers, etc. This printed circuit is designed to process a particular type of data. Some expansion cards contain their own processor (computer chip), memory, and data input and output circuits. The expansion cards are housed in the computer case. The main computer board (motherboard) offers special slots for expansion cards, as you will see on the next page. There are many types of cards; the best known are unquestionably sound cards (for the input/output of sound), graphic display adapters (which transmit information to the screen), 3D cards (designed to process 3D images such as filtering, positioning, rendering, perspective correction, texture application, smoothing, etc.), video capture cards (which convert analogue images into digital signals) and modem cards (that connect to the telephone line and allow you to access the Internet, for example).

TIP

Be careful when handling expansion cards. Never put your fingers on the connectors that fit into the slot (the protrusion formed by alternating green and golden lines). Oxidation can damage such equipment. Similarly, avoid touching the protruding elements. Always handle the cards by holding them between your thumb and index finger, making sure that you only touch the plastic parts.

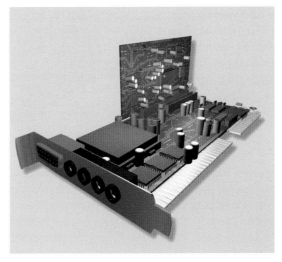

Physically installing an expansion card

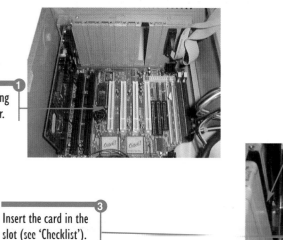

Open the housing of the computer.

Insert the card in the slot (see 'Checklist').

Remove the small protective bar of a free slot.

Replace the housing, connect the peripheral (where required) and restart the PC.

Warning!
There are two types of expansion slots — AGP and PCI. Altough it is obvious from the size of the connection strip which slot your card will fit into, it is important to check that you have a slot free for the type of card you intent to buy.

Checklist

1. Unplug all cables and open the housing of the computer.

2. Find a free slot and unscrew the corresponding small metal bar that protects the computer from dust (at the back of the PC).

3. Insert the expansion card in the free slot. To do this properly, put it at a 45° angle in the slot, start inserting it, and then press it down into the horizontal position. During this operation, use your spare hand to keep in continuous contact with the metal housing of the PC in order to prevent any discharge of static electricity.

4. Replace the housing.

5. Connect the peripherals (see p.40).Restart the computer. If the new card is not detected automatically by Windows, load the required driver using the *Add/Remove Hardware* option in the *Control Panel*.

Installing a card is an operation anyone can do. It usually works! However, the free slot may not be compatible, you may insert the card improperly (in which case the computer may not even restart), you may replace the housing incorrectly (whence annoying fan noises or vibrations), etc. In short: just follow the instructions given on this page. Proceed to install the software as indicated on the subsequent pages. And if it does not work... contact your dealer!

Checklist

To access the modem settings, for example, you must open the *Control Panel*.

1 Click *Start* and select *Settings*. A sub-menu appears.

2 Select *Control Panel*.

3 A window containing many icons is open. Behind each icon lies a dialog box related to the topic represented by the icon.

Open the Control Panel

Start/Settings/Control Panel

2 Select Control Panel.

3 Click the icon whose settings you wish to change.

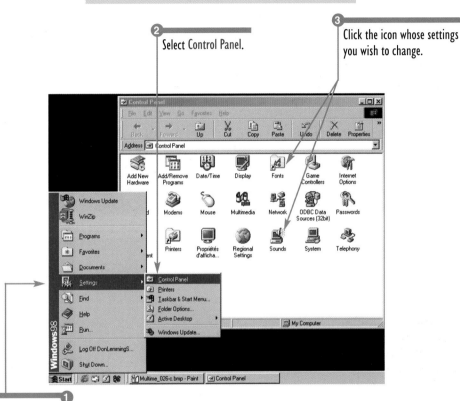

1 Select Settings.

The Control Panel is the Windows customisation control centre. From the Control Panel, you can access the system settings without difficulty: screen resolution and background colour through the Display icon, sound management through the Sounds icon, system date and time with the Date/Time icon, settings of the peripherals installed with the System icon, etc.). Through specific dialog boxes, you have access to the settings of the topics illustrated by the icons. We will keep coming back to the Control Panel throughout this book.

Conflicts between peripherals

All peripherals are managed by the computer, which delegates part of the work to the expansion cards, depending on their speciality. This means that the system must share its resources among the different peripherals while giving dialogue priorities to the expansion cards. The more peripherals you have, the greater the danger of conflicts between two or more of them. The source of a conflict usually stems from two peripherals with a similar function that have difficulties in sharing the same system resources. The most obvious symptom of a conflict is the complete disappearance of processing. A conflict between cards, for instance, may result in the loss of sound after a new expansion card has been installed. This is not always a cause for alarm. Windows has a 'Device Manager'. Thanks to this tool, you have a list of the system components, the connected peripherals and, most importantly, their operational state. This tool will often help you solve the problem, but there are so many possibilities for problems that we cannot give you a miracle formula. On the other hand, it will undoubtedly help you determine the source of the problem.

TIP

To avoid conflicts, acquire as far as possible a specific peripheral for each medium. Avoid for example sound-fax-modem cards, which are less efficient than two independent cards (a sound card and a fax-modem card). If you do buy a sound-fax-modem card nonetheless, avoid changing your mind and subsequently purchasing a better sound card while keeping the 'fax-modem' features of the current card. It is important to stick to this principle, even if at a particular time, combined peripherals do not cause any apparent problem.

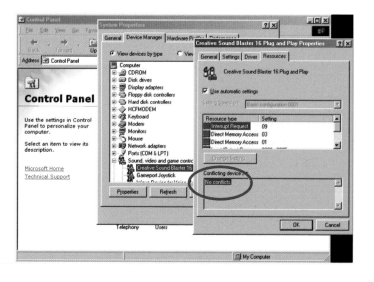

Checklist

Click the *System* icon in the *Control Panel*, and then select the *Device Manager* tab. This window pulls up a list of peripherals attached to your PC. The presentation of this list resembles that of files in the Explorer.

1 Click the ' + ' sign to expand a branch of the tree to display, for example, the list of multimedia devices (video, sound and game controllers).

2 To collapse a branch, click the ' - ' sign.

3 To access the properties and control buttons of a given peripheral, select it (click on its icon).

4 Once the device is selected, click *Properties* to access the properties dialog box (see next pages).

5 Click *Refresh* to update the hardware list. This is particularly useful if you have installed new components or if a conflict occurred that was not immediately reported by the Device Manager.

System properties

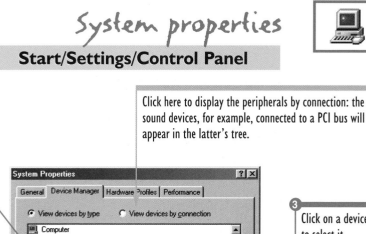

Start/Settings/Control Panel

Click here to display the peripherals by connection: the sound devices, for example, connected to a PCI bus will appear in the latter's tree.

1 Click on this sign to develop a branch.

2 Click on this sign to reduce a branch.

3 Click on a device to select it.

4 Click on this button to access the properties of the selected device.

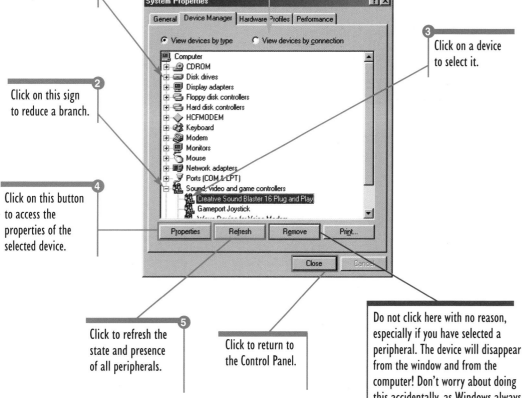

5 Click to refresh the state and presence of all peripherals.

Click to return to the Control Panel.

Do not click here with no reason, especially if you have selected a peripheral. The device will disappear from the window and from the computer! Don't worry about doing this accidentally, as Windows always ask you to confirm the removal through a warning message.

General device properties

Properties button, page 37

This button displays the device status (in case of a problem, the type of problem and a possible solution, or an error number to communicate to the manufacturer's helpdesk) as well as its main characteristics: device type, name of the manufacturer, hardware version. It also contains two tick options to be used with caution (see box).

General information on the device.

Device status: here, the device is working properly. But the message could also mention a conflict…

Click OK to return to the preceding window while accepting any changes.

You can disable a device temporarily. In this case, after it has been restarted, Windows will consider that the device is no longer part of the system. You can, however, enable it again by unticking this option. With this method you can check the effect of a device on the overall operation of the computer (or on a minor conflict). If you disable it and everything is working properly whereas nothing worked when it was enabled, reinstall the device (or keep it disabled).

Driver tab

Basic device and driver details.

Click to view the files used by the driver.

Click to update the driver (replace the current version by a more recent version).

This window grants access to information concerning the device driver. A driver is a small program which establishes the connection between the computer and a device. This program tells the computer about the presence of the device by indicating its characteristics. Each device therefore needs a driver. As there are often several versions of the same driver (each version improving or correcting errors of its predecessor), it is worth regularly checking the manufacturer's website for the most up-to-date version of the driver.

Driver File Details

This list displays the names of the files used by an active driver— a practical feature, as it enables you to view at once the essential files (which you can find on the Windows 98 CD-ROM or on the device installation disk). Windows displays missing files in lower case (as in the case of the third file in the list).

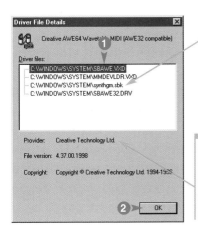

Missing file (displayed in lower case).

Windows displays the name of the provider, the file version (see the note about the drivers), and the copyright information.

Checklist

1. To access the information concerning a file, click on its name to select it.

2. Click OK to close the dialogue box.

Click the *Update Driver* button if you have a more recent version of the driver. You call a wizard like the one presented here. It looks just like a new device installation procedure. All you have to do is follow the procedure. Warning! Be ready with the proper driver on CD-ROM, on diskette, or on the hard disk if you have downloaded it from the Internet. Windows will ask you for the location of this driver.

Update drivers

Update driver button

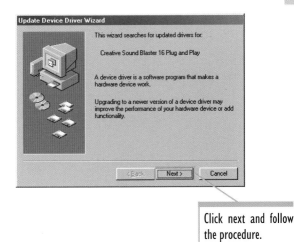

Click next and follow the procedure.

Device installation is explained on the next pages. Don't skip them...

Adding new hardware

The software installation for a new device always follows the physical installation described on page 34. There are two possible options for this installation. Either you let Windows control the situation, or you proceed with a manual installation. In the first case, Windows will use the Plug and Play approach to search for the new device. Once the scanner or the modem is detected, it will search in its own directories for the appropriate driver (Windows 98 contains drivers for nearly 1000 devices of all makes!). If the appropriate driver cannot be found on the Windows 98 disk, you will be asked to insert the disk that was supplied with the hardware. This method is recommended if you prefer not to have too much to do and if your device is a standard (a **US Robotics** modem, a **SoundBlaster** sound card, a **3D Matrox** card are standards... a Kismaï joystick far less so...). If you know how to install a device, then proceed manually: the installation will usually be faster. Just follow the steps outlined in this section.

HOW TO

The command that starts the installation process is in the Control Panel. Double-click the Add New Hardware icon.

TIP

Windows will ask you to restart the computer once you have installed the device so as to update its registry base and initialisation files.

When you click on the *Add New Hardware* icon, a window is displayed (see page 42) that asks you to close any other program. Do so, if necessary, then return to installation. Click *Next*. The next screen informs you that Windows is going to search for the new device (see page 42). Click *Next* again. Windows then displays a list of devices in conflict or incompletely installed (see page 42). Click *No*. Finally, Windows informs you that it will search for new devices.

1 Click *Yes* (Recommended) for Windows to search for the new device.

2 Click *Next* to go to the next window.

3 Windows informs you that it will now search for a new device. Click *Next*.

4 Windows searches for the new device. The scroll bar indicates the progress of the search.

Hardware installation (non PnP)

Add New Hardware

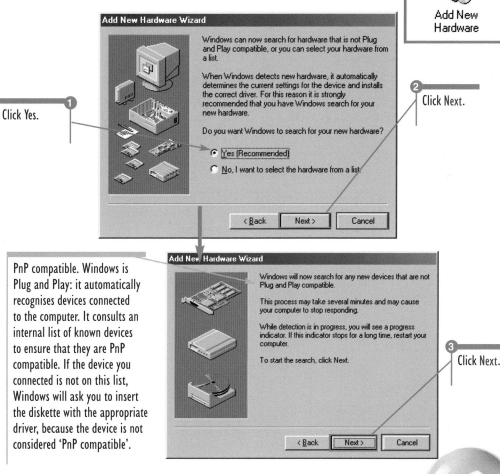

Click Yes.

Click Next.

PnP compatible. Windows is Plug and Play: it automatically recognises devices connected to the computer. It consults an internal list of known devices to ensure that they are PnP compatible. If the device you connected is not on this list, Windows will ask you to insert the diskette with the appropriate driver, because the device is not considered 'PnP compatible'.

Click Next.

To avoid errors, Windows asks for several confirmations before starting the installation of the new device. In the case of an automatic installation, you have almost nothing to do: just let Windows take care of the installation… unless it cannot find the required drivers, in which case you need to provide them.

Dialogue boxes for the installation of new hardware

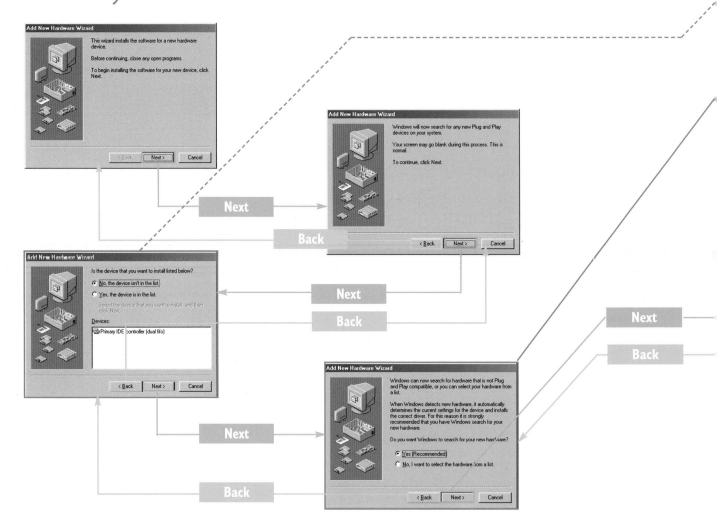

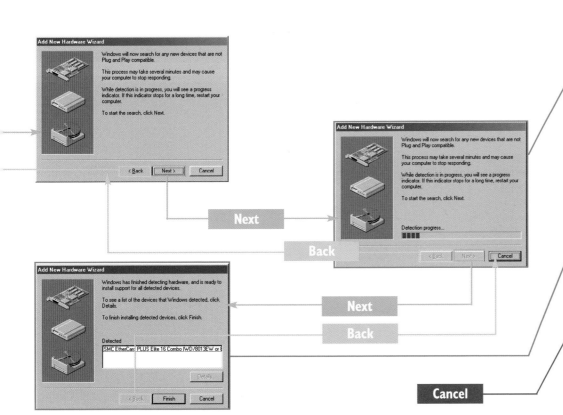

Click *Yes* if the device to install is in the list. Select it, and then click *Next*. Otherwise click *No*, then *Next*.

Click *Yes* for Windows to search for new devices. This operation may take several minutes. If the progress indicator stops for too long (more than 5 minutes), restart the computer.

Windows displays a conclusion window. Click *Details* to display the detected devices. Click *Finish* for Windows to install the drivers. If no device was detected, start the installation again and proceed manually.

Before installing the software, Windows displays a last confirmation screen with the list of detected devices.

Click to return to the *Control Panel* without installing.

Manual hardware installation

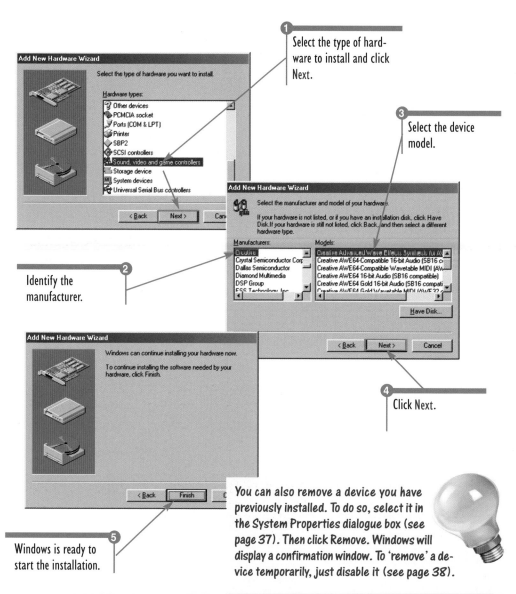

① Select the type of hardware to install and click Next.

③ Select the device model.

② Identify the manufacturer.

④ Click Next.

⑤ Windows is ready to start the installation.

You can also remove a device you have previously installed. To do so, select it in the System Properties dialogue box (see page 37). Then click Remove. Windows will display a confirmation window. To 'remove' a device temporarily, just disable it (see page 38).

Checklist

The manual installation of hardware bypasses the automatic detection scheme of Windows. You then need to specify the type of hardware you wish to install, and the path to the driver. As indicated in the previous pages, the beginning of the procedure is the same as for the automatic installation. We will therefore resume the procedure from the red dot at the top of page 41. This time we will click No rather than Yes, as described below.

① Click *No, I want to select the hardware from a list*, and then select the type of hardware to install (in our example, 'Sound, video and game controllers', for the installation of a sound card).

② On the left, identify the hardware manufacturer.

③ On the right, select the model.

④ Click *Next*.

⑤ Windows is ready to install the hardware.

Installing a new program

Installing new programs from a **CD-ROM** became much easier with Windows 95 and its **Autoplay** system. Autoplay is a feature that runs a program automatically from a **CD-ROM**, without intervention from the user. It is often used to launch installation programs. Just insert the **CD** in the drive, give it a few seconds, and Windows asks you to proceed with the installation. Alas, this only works with **CD-ROM** (and **DVD-ROM**, of course). For other media (diskettes, programs downloaded from the Internet, etc.), you have to launch the installation program manually. This program is often called either 'Setup.exe' or 'Install.exe'; the file name extension (.exe) indicates that it is an executable file, i.e. a program and not a document. An executable file can be run by double-clicking on its icon in Explorer or through the *Run* command located in the *Start Up* menu.

HOW TO

To run the installation program from a game on a diskette, for example.

1. Click Start/Run.

2. Click Browse.

3. Locate the file on the a: drive.

4. Double-click the executable file.

5. Click OK.

TIP

If the disk contains two programs entitled Install and Setup, select Install and run it. Usually in such a case, Setup is a settings program. Games, for example, are often accompanied by both an installation program and a setup program. Setup is then used to adjust musical settings (choice of sound card, etc.), display, etc.

Dialogue boxes for the manual installation of new hardware

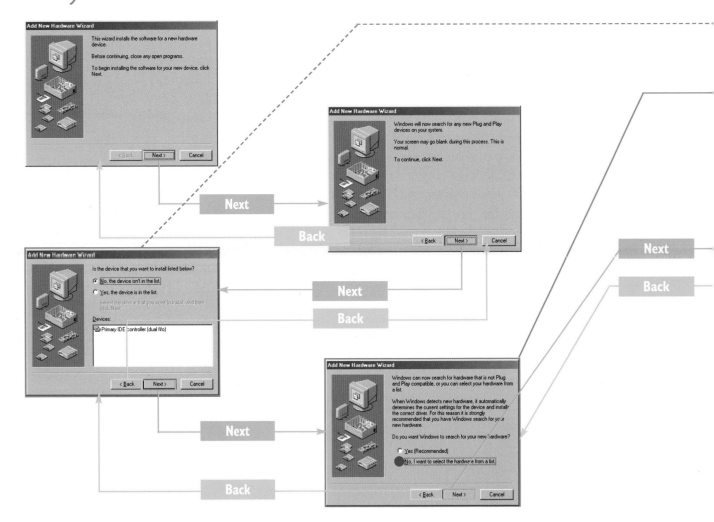

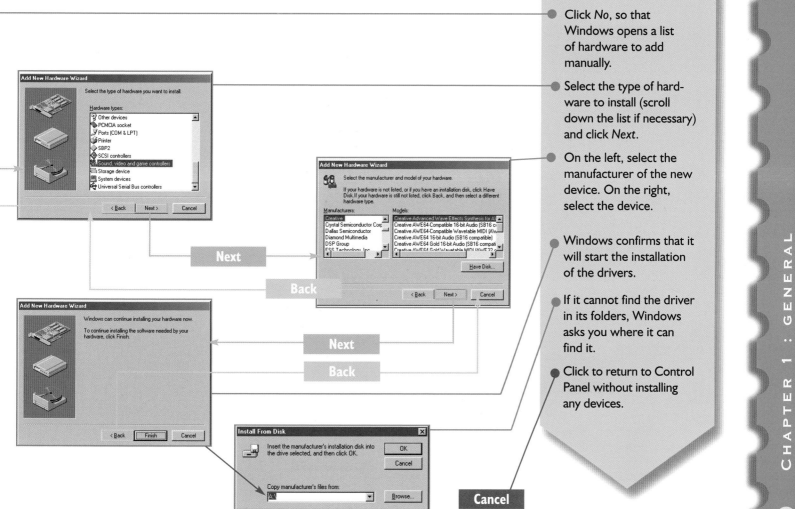

Click *Yes* if the device to install is in the list. Select it, and then click *Next*. Otherwise click *No*.

Click *No*, so that Windows opens a list of hardware to add manually.

Select the type of hardware to install (scroll down the list if necessary) and click *Next*.

On the left, select the manufacturer of the new device. On the right, select the device.

Windows confirms that it will start the installation of the drivers.

If it cannot find the driver in its folders, Windows asks you where it can find it.

Click to return to Control Panel without installing any devices.

Launching the installation procedure manually

Start/Run

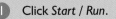

Enter the path and name for the installation file.

Click Start / Run.

Click OK.

Checklist

Let us take for example the installation of programs delivered with the SoundBlaster AWE 64 sound card.

1 Click *Start / Run*.

2 Enter the path and name for the installation program located on the CD-ROM: *drive letter:\ installation program name* .exe (example : D:\setup.exe). If you don't know the file name, use the browse button to search for it.

3 Click *OK*.

4 The program's banner screen is displayed. Select the installation language required.

The installation steps

● ●

Step 1
Select the language of installation (the choice will determine the language used by the program (including the names of the commands).

Creative Labs End-User License Agreement

Please select the language in which you wish the End-User License Agreement to be displayed.

Language : English

Next >

Step 4
Specify the installation folder. This window indicates to the PC the folder in which the program will be installed. If the folder created by default is not to your liking, click *Browse* (see next page) to specify another.

Destination Directory

Setup will install Sound Blaster AWE64 Value software in the directory shown below.

To install to this directory, click Next.

To install to a different directory, click Browse and select another directory.

You can choose not to install by clicking Cancel to exit the Setup program.

Destination Directory
C:\Program Files\Creative\CTSND   Browse...

< Back   Next >   Cancel

Next step page 52

Step 3
The *Readme* file. This is usually the last step of the installation. This file contains information about last-minute changes which could not be included in the manual, as well as troubleshooting tips. Always read it before you run the program.

Step 2
License agreement!
Yes indeed, you are expected to have bought the software you install. That is why the program often displays a copy of the license agreement (your rights and obligations as user of the program). Click *Yes*, otherwise the installation process will stop.

Creative Labs End-User License Agreement

Please read the following License agreement. Press the PAGE DOWN key to see the rest of the agreement.

Creative End-User Software License Agreement
===

PLEASE READ THIS DOCUMENT CAREFULLY BEFORE OPENING THE SEALED DISK PACKAGE OR INSTALLING THE SOFTWARE. BY OPENING THE SEALED DISK PACKAGE OR INSTALLING THE SOFTWARE, YOU ARE AGREEING TO BECOME BOUND BY THE TERMS OF THIS AGREEMENT. IF YOU DO NOT AGREE TO THE TERMS OF THE AGREEMENT, PLEASE DO NOT OPEN THE SEALED DISK PACKAGE OR INSTALL THE SOFTWARE. PROMPTLY RETURN, WITHIN 15 DAYS, THE SOFTWARE, ALL RELATED DOCUMENTATION AND ACCOMPANYING ITEMS TO THE PLACE OF ACQUISITION FOR A FULL REFUND.

This is a legal agreement between you and Creative Technology Ltd.

Do you accept all the terms of the of the preceding License Agreement? If you select No, Setup will close. To install Sound Blaster AWE64 Value,you must accept this agreement.

Yes   No

View Readme File

Please read through the contents of the readme file shown below:

Sound Blaster AWE64 Value Readme File
=====================================

This file contains additional information to supplement the manual.
Please read all the sections before you proceed with the installation.

This file contains the following sections:

1. Installation
2. Uninstallation
3. DOS Environment settings
4. DOS Audio Driver Support under Windows 95 DOS Box
5. Using CREATIVE IDE CD-ROM drive in MS-DOS Mode
6. BLASTER settings under MS-DOS Mode
7. DRAM Issues
8. AWE Control Panel WaveFx

< Back   Next >   Cancel

CHAPTER 1 : GENERAL

49

Installation dialogue boxes

For an explanation of the basic steps, see pages 47 and 49. This double-page illustrates the detailed dialogue boxes.

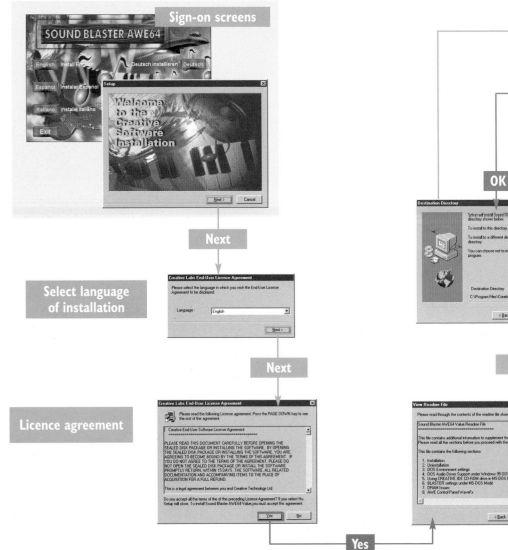

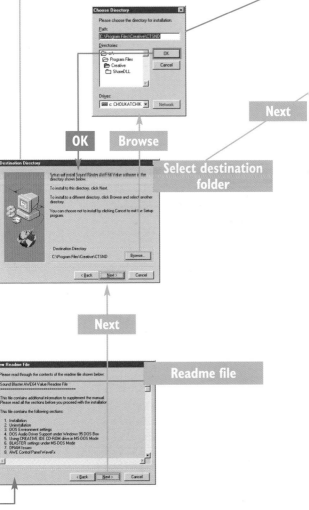

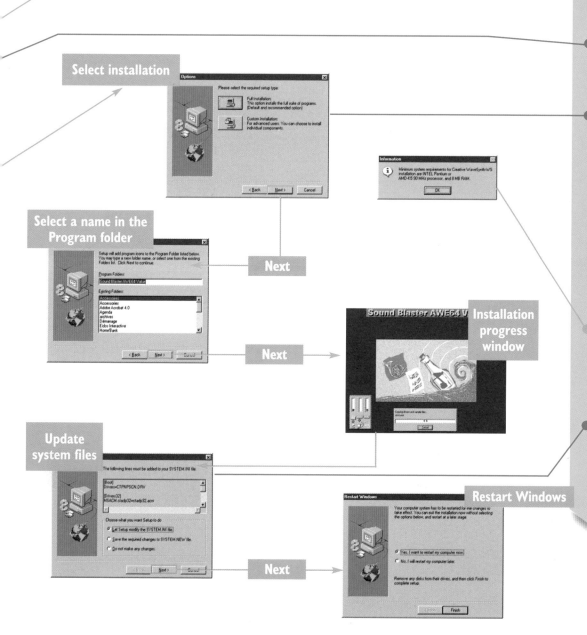

Select installation

Select a name in the Program folder

Next

Next

Update system files

Next

Sound Blaster AWE64 V

Installation progress window

Restart Windows

Click a file name or enter a path and file name at the keyboard.

Select the destination folder, then click *Next*. To select another folder, click *Browse*.

Select the type of installation. Choose a full installation if possible. A custom installation gives you the possibility of selecting the components that will be installed. In some cases, this means that you will need to insert the CD-ROM in the drive when using the application.

A message tells you about the minimum system requirements for the program.

Update system files. Click *Yes* to include the new program parameters in the system initialisation file (SYSTEM.INI).

The installation steps

Continued from page 49

Step 5 Select the type of installation, depending on your preferences and on other parameters, such as the free space available on your hard disk. When possible, select the full installation. All files are then copied onto your hard disk.

The installation process for a program may not follow the same sequence as that presented on these two pages. Some dialogue boxes may not appear at all.

Step 8 Restart.
You must often restart your computer at the final stage of the installation process, so that the changes can take effect.

Step 7 Installation.
Windows copies the required files onto the hard disk. A progress indicator is usually visible at this stage. This step takes longer when there are more files to copy.

Step 6 Program Folder.

Choose a name for the folder in which the program must be listed in the *Program Folder* (in the *Start* menu). To change the name, just type a new name in the text box or select one from the list.

Checklist

To find a file or a folder, use the *Find* command from the *Start* menu. This opens the dialog box illustrated on this page.

1. Enter the name of the file or folder you wish to find. Note that you can use wildcards (see the 'hint' box) if you do not know the exact name.

2. If possible, give Windows another clue by entering a word or a few characters that can be found in the document. Avoid commonplace (words such as 'the', 'not', 'be', etc.) that can be found in virtually all documents.

3. Specify the location to search in. In the illustration, we shall search the hard disk, but you can also limit the search to a folder.

4. Now click *Find* to start the search.

5. Windows displays the result of the search – a list of files that meet the selection criteria – in the lower part of the dialog box.

Find installed items

Start/Find/Files or Folders

The Date tab is used to find documents according to the date they were created or last modified.

The Advanced tab can be used to search according to the size and/or type of the document.

① If you know the name of the file or folder, enter it here.

④ Click to start the search.

② If possible, enter here a word that can be found in the document.

③ Specify the location to search in.

⑤ The results are displayed as a list.

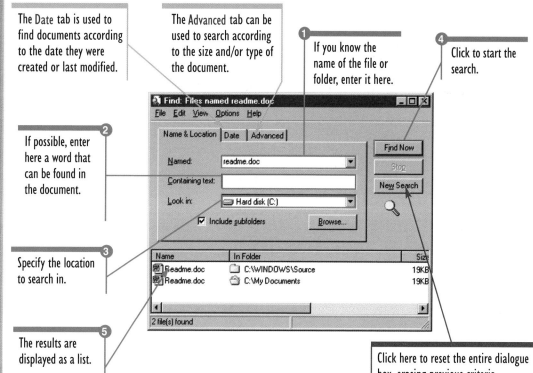

Click here to reset the entire dialogue box, erasing previous criteria. You can then start a new search.

If you can only remember part of the name of the file, use wildcard characters. These characters replace one or more letters. A question mark replaces a single letter. For example, to find a file when you don't know the first two letters of its name, enter '??voc.doc'. In this case, you are looking for a Word document (extension .doc). Similarly, an asterisk can be used instead of several missing characters. For example, car* could stand for car, carpet or carbohydrates.

![icon] Opening an installed program

Start/Programs

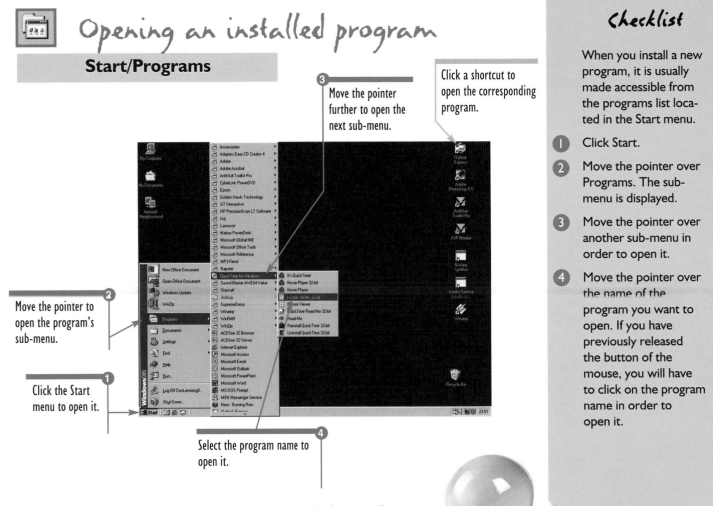

Move the pointer further to open the next sub-menu.

Click a shortcut to open the corresponding program.

Move the pointer to open the program's sub-menu.

Click the Start menu to open it.

Select the program name to open it.

Checklist

When you install a new program, it is usually made accessible from the programs list located in the Start menu.

1 Click Start.

2 Move the pointer over Programs. The sub-menu is displayed.

3 Move the pointer over another sub-menu in order to open it.

4 Move the pointer over the name of the program you want to open. If you have previously released the button of the mouse, you will have to click on the program name in order to open it.

You can also create a shortcut for a program and leave it on the Desktop. Then, you can double-click the shortcut to open the program, without using the Start menu. To create a shortcut, open the folder that contains the program, select the program icon, then click the right button of the mouse. Click the Create shortcut command. The shortcut appears in the same folder as the original icon for the program. Now drag it to the Desktop (as you did when you copied a file, see page 27). A shortcut icon always includes a small white square with a curved arrow in it.

Checklist

① In the list of software that can be removed automatically by Windows, click on the program to uninstall.

② Click *Add/Remove* to run the uninstall utility.

③ Windows asks you to confirm the uninstall procedure. This screen may be different, but the question asked remains essentially the same. Click *Yes* or *OK*.

④ Windows informs you that the uninstall procedure was carried out correctly.

⑤ Click *OK* to close the *Install/Uninstall* window.

••••• **Note** •••••

It is always recommended that you run the Windows automatic uninstallation procedure, as it deletes all traces of the program in the system files and removes the links, leaving nothing behind. In the event of a manual uninstallation (see next page), these tasks must be carried out by the user.

Uninstalling a program automatically

Add/Remove Programs

Control Panel/Add/Remove Programs

① Select the program you want to remove.

Add/Remove Programs Properties

Install/Uninstall | Windows Setup | Startup Disk

To install a new program from a floppy disk or CD-ROM drive, click Install.

[Install...]

The following software can be automatically removed by Windows. To remove a program or to modify its installed components, select it from the list and click Add/Remove.

- AntiViral Toolkit Pro for Windows 95, Windows 98 and Window
- bleem!
- DERIVE for Windows
- Matrox PowerDesk 4.10.007
- Mirabilis ICQ
- Rockwell HCF 56K Modem
- Starcraft
- WinRAR archiver
- WinZip

[Add/Remove...]

[OK] [Cancel] [Apply]

② Click to uninstall.

⑤ Click OK to return to the Control Panel.

③ Windows asks you to confirm.

Uninstall WinRAR

(?) Continue with uninstall WinRAR

[Yes] [No]

Uninstall WinRAR

(i) Uninstall completed
You should delete C:\WINRAR\UNINSTALL.EXE manually

[OK]

④ Windows informs you that the program has been successfully removed.

Some programs do not appear in the list, but have their own removal utility. This is usually located in the Programs folder, not far from the program. If you launch a removal wizard, the steps followed will not be the same as those described on this page, but they will resemble a reverse installation. Just follow the steps.

Removing a program manually

Contextual menu / Delete

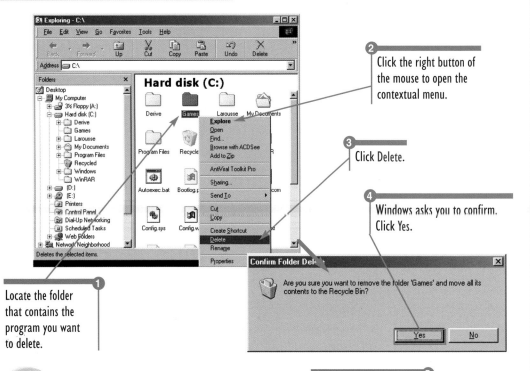

Click the right button of the mouse to open the contextual menu.

Click Delete.

Windows asks you to confirm. Click Yes.

Locate the folder that contains the program you want to delete.

Click the right button on the shortcut on the Desktop and then click Empty Recycle Bin.

A program may not appear in the list illustrated on page 55. This is probably a program you did not install with the assistance of a Wizard (see page 49), but simply by copying it in Explorer and running it. These are usually old programs, downloaded from the Internet or small programs, on a diskette. In such a case, you must proceed to a manual removal. This kind of removal always leaves traces: you delete the core of the program without necessarily deleting the links, information in the system files etc. You can, at any rate, delete any shortcuts to the program.

Checklist

1. Open Windows Explorer and find the folder containing the program folder.

2. Click the folder to select it (note that you wish to delete the entire folder, i.e. the program and all the secondary files). Then click the right button to display the contextual menu.

3. Click *Delete*.

4. Windows asks you to confirm that you want to send the folder to the *Recycle Bin*. Click *Yes*.

5. The folder is removed to the *Recycle Bin*. On the Desktop, select it, open the contextual menu by clicking with the right mouse button, and click the *Empty Recycle Bin* to delete the program.

Chapter 2

Sound

Sound level (in decibels)	Source
20 dB	whisper
35 dB	quiet bedroom
65 dB	conversation 1 metre away
70 dB	inside a car at 50 km/h
80 dB	orchestra, inside a car at high speed
90 dB	diesel lorry at 7 metres, pneumatic drill
100 dB	factory, train
120 dB	thunder, engine room of a submarine, Walkman at full blast
140 dB	jet plane on take-off
160 dB	rifle at 30 centimetres

Characteristics of an analogue sound

Sound is propagated through the air in waves similar to those that are formed and ripple away when a stone is thrown into water. When the sound wave reaches and crosses the auditory canal to hit the eardrum, the latter vibrates and transmits the characteristics of the sound heard to the nerve cells through the ossicles of the middle ear.

Sound is defined by three parameters, i.e. its frequency, intensity and tone. The frequency is the pitch of the sound: a high frequency corresponds to a high-pitched sound. This frequency is measured as the number of cycles per time unit (i.e. the number of vibrations per second). It is expressed as the Hertz (Hz). A Hertz corresponds to one cycle per second, 100 kiloHertz (kHz) correspond to 100000 cycles per second, etc. The human ear can hear sounds in the range of 20 Hz (very low) to 20000 Hz (very high-pitched sound, at the threshold of ultrasound).

The intensity of the sound is the volume of the sound. On the diagram of a sound wave, the intensity is represented by the amplitude of the curve (i.e. the 'height' of its peaks). The intensity of a sound is measured in decibels (dB). The human ear supports a sound of 140 db maximum. Beyond this limit, sound can hurt (see the table on the previous page).

Finally, the tone is produced by small interference waves that are associated with the main wave. These 'harmonic waves', as they are called, have their own frequency and intensities, allowing for fine differences in sounds. This makes it possible to differentiate an 'A' note produced with a piano from the same note played on a guitar, because the frequency of A is fixed at 440 Hz.

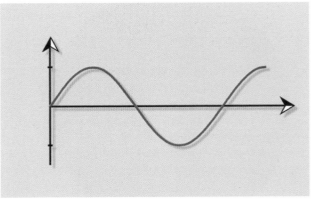

Characteristics of a digital sound

An analogue sound, as we have seen, is a wave. A digital sound, on the other hand, is not a natural sound, but is produced by electronic equipment that can only manage information in binary form (series of '0' and '1'). A digital sound therefore tends to imitate a wave by means of new characteristics: the sampling frequency (or rate) and coding. To produce a sound frequency, a computer divides each second of sound into a collection of sound samples (whence the sampling). As the number of samples increases, the sound becomes more precise (but it takes up more space on the hard disk). The unit of this 'sampling frequency' is the Hertz.

Eight bit coding requires less storage space, while 16 bit coding requires more space. Eight bit coding provides 256 values for the amplitude, which is not enough to generate a precise, realistic sound, while 16 bit coding, on the other hand, offers 65 536 values for the amplitude. The sound is a lot more realistic, but it takes up more space.

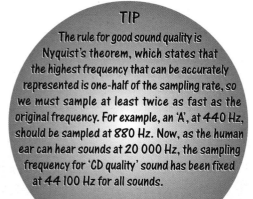

TIP
The rule for good sound quality is Nyquist's theorem, which states that the highest frequency that can be accurately represented is one-half of the sampling rate, so we must sample at least twice as fast as the original frequency. For example, an 'A', at 440 Hz, should be sampled at 880 Hz. Now, as the human ear can hear sounds at 20 000 Hz, the sampling frequency for 'CD quality' sound has been fixed at 44 100 Hz for all sounds.

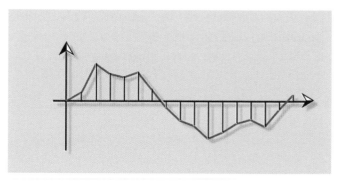

Sound equipment in a PC

The most important sound device in a **PC** is the sound card, which acts like the amplifier of a **Hi-Fi** system. The equivalent of the Hi-Fi's controls can be found in the programs that control the sound card. The sound card generates the sounds included in games, educational **CD-ROMs** and audio **CDs**. You must of course connect an output device to the card (i.e. headphones or speakers).

The sound card can also be used to record sound through a microphone. You can vary the different 'remote control' features to listen to nearly any sound. The sound card goes to work on sound, because it has an array of programs that simulate the main dials of a professional recording studio. So you have a very complete sound mixer along with a recording table to adjust the recording level of several mixed sounds.

You also may have a **MIDI** editor and a wave editor program, which are quite fun to use.

HOW TO

The collection of programs that accompany the SoundBlaster card mimics a complete sound recording studio, with its CD player, its MIDI interface controls, its sound mixer and a simple sound recording tool. It also contains a remote control.

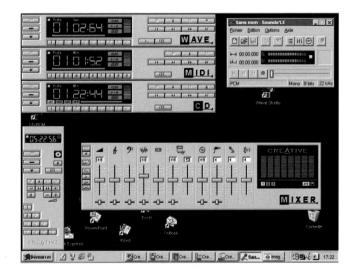

Connecting devices to a sound card

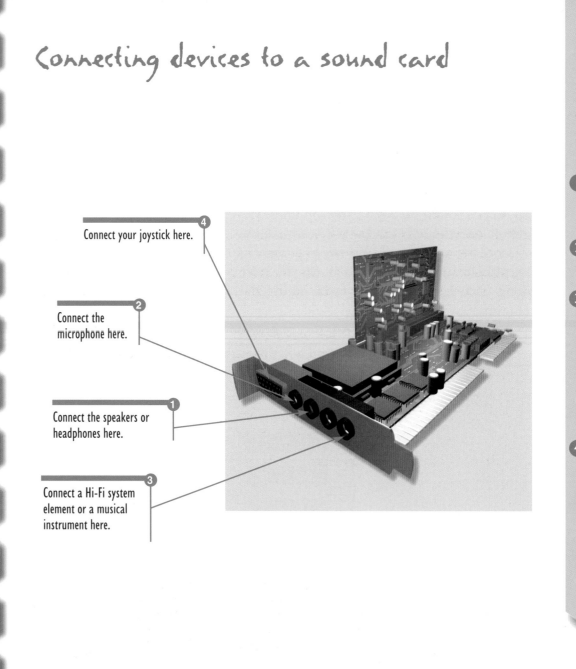

Connect your joystick here.

2 Connect the microphone here.

1 Connect the speakers or headphones here.

3 Connect a Hi-Fi system element or a musical instrument here.

Checklist

Most sound cards offer several connectors. They often include a game port to which you can connect a joystick.

1. *Line out* or *spk out* (*speaker out*) port, which can be used to connect speakers or headphones.
2. *Rec in* (record in) or *mic port* is used to connect a microphone.
3. *Line in* port, to which you can connect an amplifier, using a double-jack to mini-jack adapter. Double-jack adapters are readily available on the market (double-jacks are the red and white plugs used on Hi-Fi systems).
4. *Joy* or *joystick* port, to which you can connect your joystick or your gamepad.

Calculating the size of an audio file

The size of a sound file varies according to four parameters: the (time) length, the sampling frequency, the coding, and the number of channels. The length of the piece obviously affects the final size. A one-minute piece will be a fifth of the size of a five-minute equivalent. The sampling frequency is fundamental: the higher the frequency, the greater the accuracy, but the larger the file. The file size is multiplied fivefold or more when going from 8 bit coding to 16 bit coding. Finally, the number of channels (mono or stereo) also influences the file size, doubling it when going from mono to stereo.

Two factors must be considered when selecting the coding: the frequency and the number of channels for a sound. First, consider the destination of the sound. It is useless to produce CD-quality sound when the sound will be played on an FM radio: the sampling frequency of the latter is limited to 22 050 Hz whereas the CD is sampled at 44 100 Hz, fifty percent of the data would be redundant. The second factor is the space available on the disks.

You can calculate the size of a sound file on the basis of the four parameters. Imagine a 3 min. 20 sec. sound of CD-quality, coded in 16 bits. Multiply these parameters to find out the size of the file: 200 s x 172 kb/s = 34 400 kb or, if you prefer a result in bits:

200 (seconds) x 16 (bits) x 44 100 (Hz) x 2 (channels) = 282 240 000 bits. Divide this number by 8 to obtain the number of bytes (as 1 byte = 8 bits), i.e. 35 280 000 bytes. Divide the result by 1024 to express it in kilobytes.

This gives 34 453, 125 kb., i.e. more than 34 Mb on your hard disk!

Destination and free space				
Channels	Coding	Frequency	Weight in kb/second	Use
Mono	8 bits	8 000 Hz	8 kb/s	Telephone
Mono	8 bits	11 025 Hz	11 kb/s	AM Radio
Stereo	16 bits	22 050 Hz	86 kb/s	FM Radio
Stereo	16 bits	44 100 Hz	172 kb/s	CD
Stereo	16 bits	48 000 Hz	187 kb/s	DAT

The different audio file formats

There are very few audio file formats (whereas there are many image formats). This means that audio programs are usually compatible with most common audio formats, at least within a specific environment (PC, Macintosh, Unix, etc.). Note that audio files are often large documents. Many users save space on their hard disk by compressing their audio files with specialised software (Sox, Aware...), which uses a compression algorithm to detect blocks of repetitive data within the file and to record them in a more efficient way.

Finally, a distinction must be drawn between purely audio formats and mixed formats, such as e.g. video formats (where sound is usually synchronised with the image) which can be used without image.

Audio files

WAVE (extension .WAV)
Windows format. Compatible with virtually any program that deals with sound (including office automation applications that can work with sound).

Audio Interchange File Format (extension : AIFF)
More specific to the Macintosh environment, these files can usually be read by programs under Windows. Also available with compression (the extension then becomes AIFC).

Audio-μLaw (extension .AU)
Audio format used on Unix platforms: of medium quality (8-bit coding). Main advantage: generates relatively small files, hence its success on the Internet.

Mixed formats

Digital module (extension .MOD)
Hybrid files that contain sound and instructions on how it has to be reproduced (like a **MIDI** file; see below). Widely used.

QuickTime
Developed by Apple for its Macintosh, QuickTime files can integrate sound, MIDI instructions, text, video – all encoded on perfectly synchronised tracks. If the software is on the computer, it can also be used as a compression utility.

MP3
Initially used for video, **MPEG 1** and **2** formats led to MP3, which compresses **CD** quality sound to $1/12^{th}$ of the original size. It is now the main format used on the Internet.

The properties dialogue box of a sound file informs you about its file format, its location and the space the file uses on the disk. More information is available when using the contextual menu that is shown for the file when using Explorer.

1. In the Windows Explorer window, select the sound file.

2. Click the icon with the right button of the mouse, then select *Properties*.

3. Windows opens the *Properties* dialogue box.

4. You can check the file format, the precise path to reach it and the file size.

5. Click *OK* to close the *Properties* window and return to the Explorer window.

Accessing sound file properties

Contextual menu/Properties

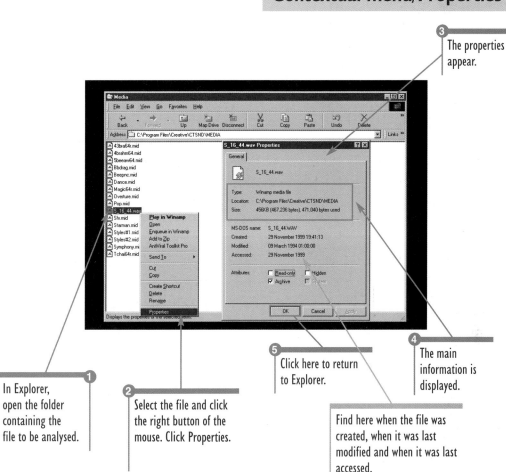

3 The properties appear.

4 The main information is displayed.

5 Click here to return to Explorer.

Find here when the file was created, when it was last modified and when it was last accessed.

1 In Explorer, open the folder containing the file to be analysed.

2 Select the file and click the right button of the mouse. Click Properties.

65

Checklist

1. The 'Details' tab is very important: it provides information about the format of the sound: coding, sampling frequency, and number of channels used.

2. It also displays the length of the piece. In our example, the sound is very short: just 0.46 second.

3. Click *OK* to return to Explorer.

File details

Details tab

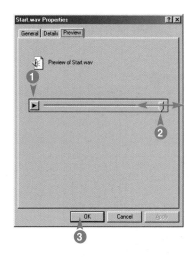

This tab also tells you whether the sound is protected by a copyright. If so, you cannot use it freely. However, the absence of a copyright notice does not automatically imply that the file is not under copyright. The notice could have been removed by manipulation. A small audio file (less than 3 seconds), such as the one in the illustration, cannot be copyrighted.

Preview tab

You do not need to open the Properties dialogue box to listen to the sound: just double-click its icon in Explorer to launch the playback program (we shall discuss this program in the next section).

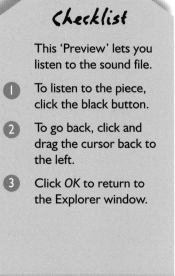

Checklist

This 'Preview' lets you listen to the sound file.

1. To listen to the piece, click the black button.

2. To go back, click and drag the cursor back to the left.

3. Click *OK* to return to the Explorer window.

Windows 98 and sound

Windows 98 is a multimedia-oriented operating system. Its basic version therefore contains a collection of multimedia programs, including some special sound management tools. The Volume Control enables you to adjust the output volume. It can also be used as a sound mixer. The Sound Recorder can be used to record sounds and to create special effects.

If you wish to customise your computer, you can tell Windows which audio files (those you have recorded, a clip from a CD, a jingle downloaded from the Internet etc.) to play for events such as the opening or closing of Windows, errors, etc.

HOW TO

You can call the Volume Control program from the taskbar. Click the button illustrated with a speaker. This opens a simple Volume Control window. Move the cursor up or down, in order to increase or decrease the volume.

Setting up the sound card

Multimedia folder

Checklist

① Click the *Multimedia* icon in the *Control Panel* and select the *Audio tab*.

② Windows displays the default (preferred) device for playback and for recording.

③ Click here to access the advanced playback properties dialogue box.

④ Click to access the advanced recording properties dialogue box.

⑤ Click to access the playback volume control dialogue box (sound mixer).

⑥ Click to access the Sound Recorder.

⑦ Click OK to close this window and return to the *Control Panel*.

⑤ Click to access the Volume Control tool.

① Click the Audio tab.

② Windows displays the devices used for sound.

③ Click to access the advanced playback properties.

④ Click to access the advanced recording properties.

⑥ Click to access the Sound Recorder.

⑦ Click to close this window, and save all changes.

Tick this box to display the Volume Control icon on the status bar (see 'How To' on previous page).

Multimedia Properties

Audio | Video | MIDI | CD Music | Devices

Playback
Preferred device:
SB16 Wave Out [240]
To select advanced options, click: Advanced Properties

Recording
Preferred device:
SB16 Wave In [240]
To select advanced options, click: Advanced Properties

☐ Use only preferred devices.
☑ Show volume control on the taskbar.

OK | Cancel | Apply

When Windows has detected your sound card, it integrates it in the Device Manager window (see page 37). It should do the same in the multimedia Device Manager window. This window gives you access to various controls and advanced properties of the sound recording and reproduction programs.

If you have several sound cards in your PC, click the down pointing arrow attached to the Preferred device text box. You will then see a list of all devices available.

Advanced audio properties

Speakers tab

You can find on the market 'Dolby Surround Stereo' systems with five speakers (one for each side of the screen, two behind your desk chair, and a base woofer under the screen, for example). With such devices, the reproduction of sound is excellent and you benefit from a better identification of sound (left, right, behind you, etc.). Perfect for games such as Duke Nukem, Quake, etc., in which the player is immersed in a stressful universe. Note however that most of these systems are connected to the PC via a USB port.

Checklist

To select the type of speakers you are using :

1. Click the down arrow to display the list of options.

2. Select your particular Set up.

3. Click OK to save the changes and return to the Control Panel.

Performance tab

Checklist

1. If the system is not working properly, it may be because of hardware acceleration. Move the slide bar to the left to slow everything down.

2. If the system slows down or stops responding when you try to convert an audio file, move the slide bar to the left. The conversion quality will decline, but the system will accelerate.

3. Click OK to return to the Control Panel.

The conversion is similar to the translation from an analogue signal to a digital signal (see beginning of this chapter). For the sampling frequency to approach 44100 Hz, you must move the slide bar as far as possible to the right. If your PC slows down, reduce the sampling frequency. This, of course, will reduce the quality of the conversion by the same proportion.

Audio setup flow chart

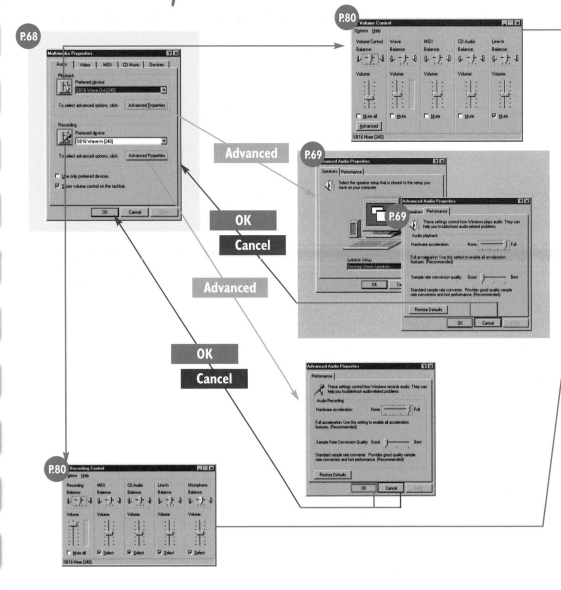

Sound mixer

Used to mix playback sounds (see page 80).

Recording sound mixer

Used to control the recording input level (see page 81).

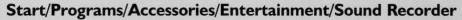

Checklist

1. Once you have opened the *Sound Recorder*, click *File/Open* and find the file on the disk using the usual procedure (see Chapter 01, if necessary).

2. Click on the play button to listen to the sound or to resume listening after a pause.

3. Click the stop button to stop.

4. Drag the sliding cursor with the left button of the mouse to go backwards or forwards. The line represents the length of the sound as a time line. The position of the sliding cursor is indicated in seconds in the left part of the window.

5. Click the exit button to close the Program.

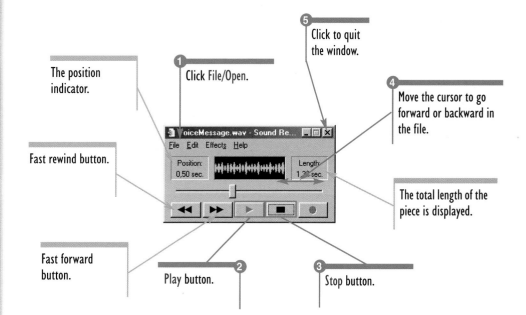

⑤ Click to quit the window.

The position indicator.

① Click File/Open.

④ Move the cursor to go forward or backward in the file.

Fast rewind button.

The total length of the piece is displayed.

Fast forward button.

② Play button.

③ Stop button.

To listen to an audio file from Explorer, just double-click its icon. Another window will open, in this case ActiveMovie. To open the single menu available, click with the right button of the mouse on the position indicator.

Control sound volume

Start/Programs/Accessories/Entertainment/Volume control

To decrease the volume, drag the slide bar down.

To increase the volume, drag the slide bar up.

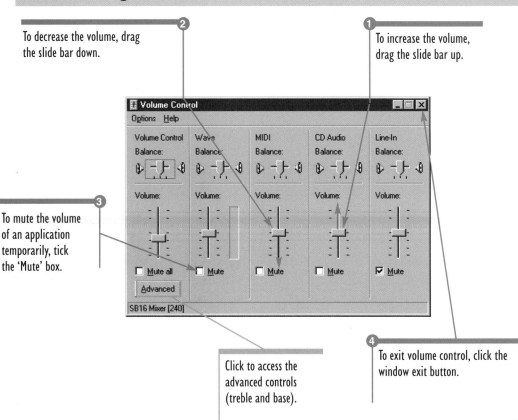

To mute the volume of an application temporarily, tick the 'Mute' box.

Click to access the advanced controls (treble and base).

To exit volume control, click the window exit button.

Do not be intimidated in front of this collection of slide bars, but do read the box below. This application has its own output volume controled by two slide bars: balance and volume. The volume slide bar controls the sound volume. The balance (horizontal) slide bar controls the proportion of sound transmitted to the right and left speakers. When centred, this cursor indicates that the sound is balanced: the right and left speakers 'output' the same volume. If, for example, the left speaker is much closer to your ear than the right one, you might reduce its volume and increase the volume of the right speaker by dragging the sliding cursor to the right.

Each column controls the output of a different sound source: a connected device (Line-in), the audio CD Player, the MIDI applications, the Wave program installed at the same time as the sound card and, on the far left, the general output volume. Other columns can appear, such as special features of your sound card. The general output volume is the volume transmitted to the speakers (independently from their own volume control). The output volume of the Audio drive is the volume at the output of the drive, which is then transmitted to the sound card, etc.

Adjusting the tone

Advanced button, page 72

Advanced Controls for Volume Control

These settings can be used to make fine adjustments to your audio.

Tone Controls

These settings control how the tone of your audio sounds.

Bass: Low ————————— High

Treble: Low ————————— High

Other Controls

These settings make other changes to how your audio sounds. See your hardware documentation for details.

☐ 1 3D Stereo Enhancement

Close

Tick this option if you have 'Dolby Surround Stereo' or if you wish to generate 3D sound with other types of speakers (in which case, the quality of the result cannot be guaranteed).

Checklist

1. To increase the bass, drag the sliding cursor to the right.

2. To reduce the treble, drag the sliding cursor to the left.

3. Click *Close* to save the changes.

Checklist

If you are using only three applications (for example, Audio CD, MIDI drive and microphone), you can mask the other slide bars.

1. Click *Options/Properties*.

2. Under '*Show the following volume controls*' untick the check boxes for the devices you don't use.

3. Click *OK* to return to volume control.

Simplify the sound mixer

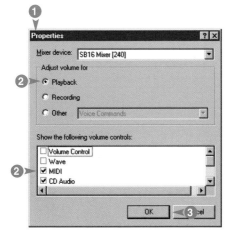

Properties

Mixer device: SB16 Mixer [240]

Adjust volume for

◉ Playback

○ Recording

○ Other   Voice Commands

Show the following volume controls:

☐ Volume Control
☐ Wave
☑ MIDI
☑ CD Audio

OK   ncel

You can also display the recording (input) volume controls from this dialogue box. Just click Recording.

Recording a sound

To record a sound, you must first play a sound (from an audio CD, a MIDI sound, or even a simple audio file). Then adjust the recording volume from the recording volume control window. Finally, open the sound recorder. The entire procedure is described on pages 77 and 78. For the moment, we shall concentrate on operating the sound recorder.

The entire procedure is described on pages 77 and 78.

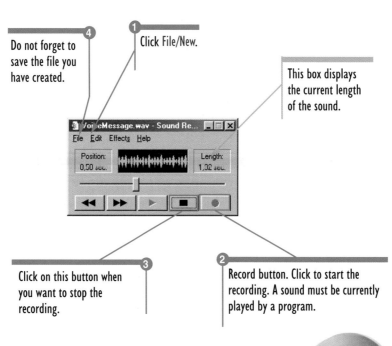

④ Do not forget to save the file you have created.

① Click File/New.

This box displays the current length of the sound.

③ Click on this button when you want to stop the recording.

② Record button. Click to start the recording. A sound must be currently played by a program.

The recorded sound uses the default settings (i.e. number of channels, sampling frequency and coding). To change the settings, click Save as, which opens a standard Save as... dialog box. Locate the Change button, which opens another dialog box through which you can change the settings. You can also open this box to convert a CD quality file or a radio quality file, for example. The conversion process is explained on the next page.

The conversion process is explained on the next page.

Checklist

① Click *File/New* to create a new audio file. You cannot record a new sound in an existing file that already contains sound.

② Click the record button as soon as you are ready to record the sound. Play the sound. The indicators display the length of the recording.

③ To stop recording, click the stop button. It is better to let the recording run a few extra seconds: this way, you will not miss anything (deleting the superfluous seconds is very simple). You can resume recording by clicking on the *Record* button.

④ When finished, do not forget to save the file with *File/Save*.

Sound Recorder/File/Properties

Checklist

1. Note the current properties of the file as you may not need to change anything!

2. Click the *Convert Now* button to access the sound settings. The 'Sound Selection' dialogue box is displayed.

3. From the *Name* menu, select an audio format (CD quality, radio quality, etc.). The *Attributes* drop-down menu instantly adopts the standard values of the chosen format.

4. You can also customise a format. In this case, make sure it is compatible with your intended destination, if you wish to output it from the PC. Click the *Attributes* menu and select more original attributes.

5. Click *OK* to return to the 'Properties' window.

1 The window displays the settings of the open file.

Properties for VoiceMessage.wav

Details

VoiceMessage.wav

Copyright: No Copyright information
Length: 1.32 sec.
Data Size: 14625 bytes
Audio Format: PCM 11.025 Hz; 8 Bit; Mono

Format Conversion

To adjust the sound quality or use less space for this sound, click Convert Now.

Choose from:

All formats | Convert Now...

OK   Cancel

2 Click to convert the file.

Sound Selection

Name:
Radio Quality | Save As...   Remove

Format: PCM
Attributes: 22.050 Hz; 8 Bit; Mono   22 KB/s

OK   Cancel

3 Select an audio format.

4 Select a customised audio format.

5 Click to return to the file properties window.

CHAPTER 2 : SOUND

75

Checklist

It is easy to delete 'blank' from a recording.

1. Move the sliding cursor to the beginning of the sound. The position of the sliding cursor is indicated in the left window.

2. Click *Edit/Delete Before Current Position*.

   An excerpt is deleted from the piece.

Deleting residual seconds

Edit/Delete Before Current Position

The same procedure can be applied to delete the blank part at the end of the sound. This time, select Edit/ Delete After Current Position. You now just have the sound you wanted to record.

Special effects

The sound recorder can apply special effects – admittedly limited, but fun – to a sound file. These effects are listed in the Effects menu. An effect is applied directly to the open file. When you save the file, the effects are also recorded.

Increase and decrease volume
Used to increase and decrease the output volume independently of the Volume Control. Increases the volume by 25% by default.

Add echo
Adds echo to the sound. Unfortunately, it is not possible to control the value of the echo, which proves a bit too intense for musical pieces, but is acceptable for voices.

Reverse
Generates a 'mirror' image of the sound, starting from the end and going backwards.

Increase and decrease speed
Used to adjust the speed at which the sound will be played. To accelerate it, select *Effects/ Increase Speed* (incremented by 100%). You can thus have the sound run at 200%. Use this effect carefully, as it is not always easy to go back to the normal speed.

Recording a track from an audio CD

Step 1

Insert an audio CD in the CD-ROM drive. This automatically calls the CD player. The next section of this book covers the Audio CD Player.

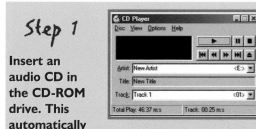

Step 2

Open the Sound Recorder and the Recording Control (*Edit/Audio Properties*). All the tools are ready to start the recording.

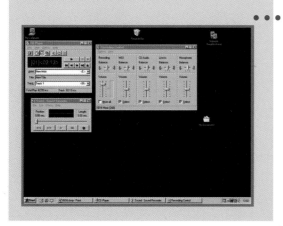

Step 3

In the Recording Control, drag the CD Audio sliding cursor to the maximum. Leave the balance control in the centre if possible. You can always adjust it subsequently when you are listening to the recorded track).

Step 4

The Sound Recorder opens a new file automatically. You can now start recording. In the CD Player window, go to the beginning of the track you want to record, and click *Pause* (see next section). You are ready to play the track.

Step 5 In the Sound Recorder window, click the Record button. Then go back to the CD Player window to start reading the track. You have recorded a few blank seconds (the time it took to go from one window to the next). The Recording Control displays the recording level.

Step 6 When the track is finished, let the Sound Recorder record a few additional seconds, then click the stop button. The length of the sound is displayed. Click the single arrow to play the sound back from the beginning.

Step 8 Repeat this procedure to delete the blank at the end of the recording. Your recording can now be saved on a disk. Click *File/Save* to complete the action.

Step 7 Drag the sliding cursor to the beginning of the sound, just after the short blank (the wave, in the centre, is flat, confirming that there is no sound). Click *Edit/Delete Before Current Position*. The Sound Recorder asks you to confirm that you want to delete part of the sound. Click *Yes* to complete the procedure.

Inserting a recorded sound into another and mixing two sound files

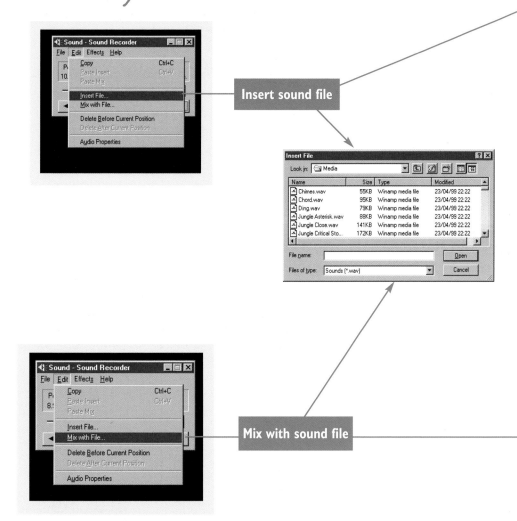

Insert sound file

Mix with sound file

Browse the disks, then select the sound file you want to insert. It will be inserted in the currently open file, at the exact location of the cursor. The two files are not mixed: the sound you insert cuts the original file sound at the insertion point, and pushes the remaining section further along.

Browse the disks, then select the sound file you want to mix with the currently open sound. This time, the two sounds will be mixed. From the location of the cursor, the listener will hear both sounds simultaneously. The total length of the file has not changed. Mixing enables you to create special effects such as adding the sound of a motorbike to background music, for example. The only problem is that the two sounds are played with the same volume. If you mix a voice that was recorded with a standard microphone with music extracted from a CD, the voice may not be very audible. This problem can be solved with the Windows Sound Mixer (Recording control) or the SoundBlaster card software.

How a sound mixer works

Start / Programs / Accessories / Entertainment / Volume Control
Or Start / Programs / SoundBlaster (or other folder) / Creative Mixer

A sound mixer is an audio instrument capable of mixing sounds from several sources (in the case of a Hi-Fi system, the **CD** player, the record deck, the cassette deck, the tuner, etc. are connected to the input jacks, while the recorder is connected to the output jack). A sound mixer is useful because it can control the volume of one sound in relation to another, depending on its source. If, for example, you want to hear a speech recorded on a cassette with a musical background coming from a **CD**, you can set the speech volume at 100% and music at 20%. If you reverse the two values, you will barely hear the speech, which will be covered by the music. If you choose to set them both at 50%, the volume will be the same for both, but the musical piece, richer and more powerful (because it is a better recording, a purer and louder) will drown out the speech. Finally, if you set both at 100%, you will get a confusion of sound and it would be difficult to distinguish the two components.

The slide bar on the left of the window is the master slide bar, which controls the output volume of the mix.

TIP
You can use either the Windows Volume Control, or the Sound Mixer program of the Sound-Blaster, as you wish, because they replicate each other. If you decide to limit yourself to small recordings, as explained in the preceding pages, then use the Windows volume control. If you wish to use all the features of your sound card, then you should work with the Creative Mixer.

Adjusting the recording level

Start / Programs / Accessories / Entertainment / Volume Control

Or Start / Programs / SoundBlaster (or other folder) / Creative Mixer

In the case of the Recording Console, the controls adjust, for each sound source, its recorded intensity. Let us say that you want to record, for example, a speech and background music as you hear it on the speakers. To do this, select the input devices you will use (e.g. the **CD Player** and the microphone).

Note that this sound mixer contains a light indicator, just like most **Hi-Fi** systems: the input level indicator. It is made up of coloured bars ranging from deep green (at the bottom) to red (at the top). This can help you adjust the volume so as to avoid track saturation: when the indicator reaches the red, the sound volume is too high. You will probably record too much bass, the sounds will get confused; the result, disappointing. To do things properly, most of the recording must remain in the green, and the peaks must not go past the first yellow bar. Do practice before recording, so that you can control the recording level. Finally, as far as possible, do not fiddle with the balance during the recording. You will produce an unbalanced sound, which is difficult to re-balance. You can always adjust the balance when playing back recorded pieces, using the Volume Control dialogue box (see previous page).

HOW TO

Drag the sliding cursors for the devices you are recording from, so that the volumes are set at an appropriate input level (not exceeding the first yellow bar).

Sound level management

Mixing two sound sources

Now you want to listen simultaneously to a piece from a CD (as background music) and to a speech you have recorded in a *.wav* file. Open the Volume Control. Select the two devices by clicking on the corresponding button illustrated with a speaker **(A)**, drag the sliding cursor for the CD up to 40% **(B)**, for example, and that of the *.wav* file to 100% **(C)**, and adjust the master output volume with the master sliding cursor **(D)** or with the speaker Volume control.

Mixing two music pieces

An interesting application of the Sound Mixer is to produce a fade-out–fade-in between the end of one piece and the beginning of the next one, so to avoid the blank that would usually separate them. Here, once again, you will use the sliding cursors. Let us suppose you have previously recorded a piece from a **CD** with the Sound Recorder (excerpt A) and you want to fade-out–fade-in with another piece coming from the **CD** Player (excerpt B). Initially, the sliding cursor for the recorded piece is at its maximum; that of the **CD** Player at the minimum. When you reach the end of excerpt A, start the **CD** Player. Now reduce the output volume of excerpt A and increase the volume of excerpt B. The sliding cursors will cross approximately half way through their course. You will hear the two sounds mix. Continue the movement: excerpt A will gradually fade out as excerpt B fades in.

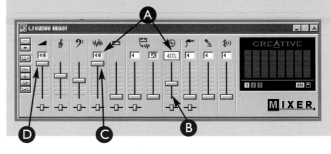

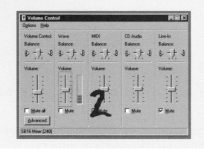

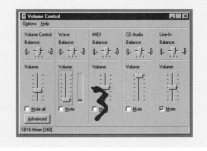

Checklist

The CD Player of Windows contains all the controls of a standard CD player in a Hi-Fi system. It can be launched from the Windows *Start* menu. Alternatively, all you have to do for the CD Player to start up is to insert an audio CD in the CD-ROM drive.

To listen to a CD

1. Click play.

2. Click stop to stop playing the piece and return to the beginning of the track. To stop temporarily and resume playing subsequently, use pause. Just click this button once again to resume playing.

3. Click the minimise button to minimise the window. The CD continues to play but does not clutter the screen.

4. To change CD, click eject. The drive drawer will open automatically.

Start/Programs/Accessories/Entertainment/CD Player

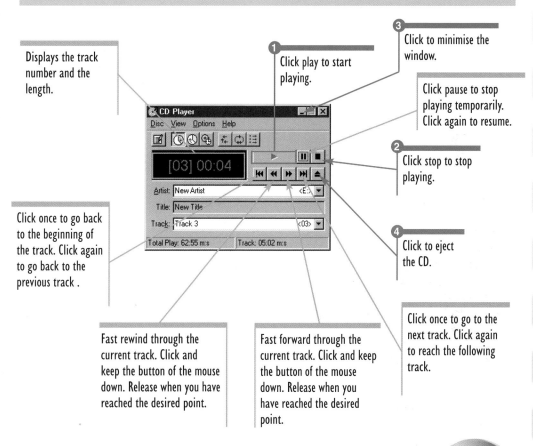

Displays the track number and the length.

① Click play to start playing.

③ Click to minimise the window.

Click pause to stop playing temporarily. Click again to resume.

② Click stop to stop playing.

Click once to go back to the beginning of the track. Click again to go back to the previous track.

④ Click to eject the CD.

Fast rewind through the current track. Click and keep the button of the mouse down. Release when you have reached the desired point.

Fast forward through the current track. Click and keep the button of the mouse down. Release when you have reached the desired point.

Click once to go to the next track. Click again to reach the following track.

If you want to stop temporarily, use the pause button; click once more on it to resume listening.

This is the standard window of the CD player. It may be slightly different depending on the display options you have selected.

The CD Player features three playing options. To display their icons, click *View/Toolbar*. These options are: 'Random order' (the tracks are played in a random order), 'Continuous play' (the CD is played endlessly in a loop, until you stop it) or 'Intro play' (you listen to the first few seconds of each track) – a particularly useful option when you want to find a track whose title you do not know.

CD Player options

CD Player, options menu

Random order.

Continuous play.

Intro play.

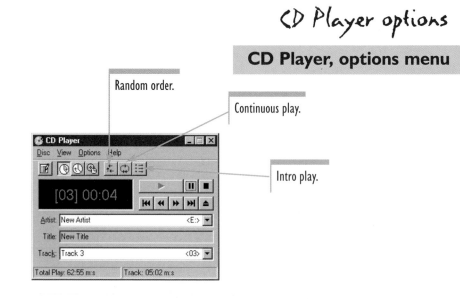

Preferences

CD Player, Options/Preferences

Specifies that the CD playing must stop when you exit the CD Player window. If the option is unticked the CD will continue to play.

Specifies that the changes made to the player (display mode, track playing options, etc.) must be saved.

Set the length of each track introduction you want to listen to when listening in 'Intro play' mode.

Choose the character size for the display of the elapsed time.

Checklist

1. Enter the name of the CD artist in the *Artist* field.

2. Enter the title of the CD in the *Title* field.

3. Click a track name ('Track 2' for example) in the *Available Tracks* field to select that track.

4. The lower text field displays the name of the selected track. Change the name (i.e. title) of the track as you wish.

5. To confirm the change, click *Set Name*. The old name is now replaced by the new name. Select the next track you want to rename and give it a new name. Repeat the procedure until all tracks have been renamed.

6. Click *OK* to confirm the changes.

Entering CD track names

Disc/Edit Playlist

Displays the selected CD Player (if you have several CD-ROM drives). Just select another player in the list if needed.

1. Click and enter the name of the artist.

2. Click and enter the title of the CD.

3. Click a track name to select it.

4. Click and replace with the new name for the selected track.

5. Click to set the name.

6. Click to confirm the changes.

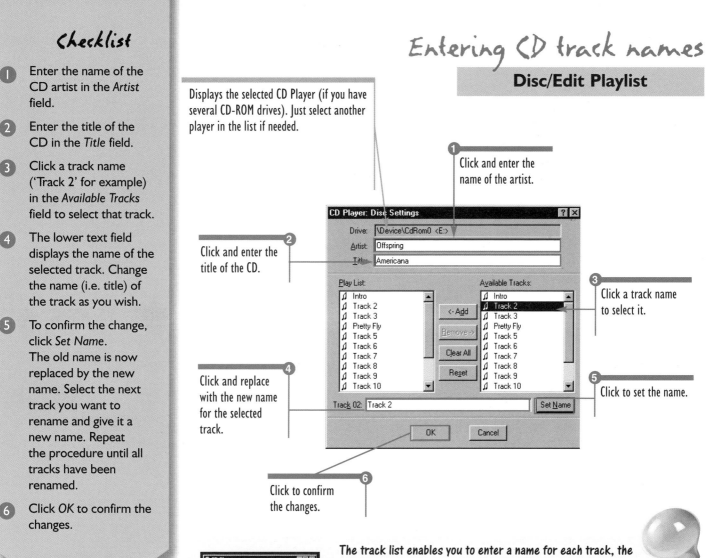

The track list enables you to enter a name for each track, the name of the artist and the title of the CD. These are displayed in the CD Player window while the CD is playing and remain in memory until you eject the CD from the drive. The titles are recorded and will appear next time you listen to the CD. This track list also enables you to program the order in which the tracks must be played, as we shall see on the next page.

CD play list

Disc/Edit play list

Click Add.

CD Player: Disc Settings

Drive: \Device\CdRom0 <E:>
Artist: Offspring
Title: Americana

Play List:
Intro
Track 2
Track 3
Pretty Fly
Track 5
Track 6
Track 7
Track 8
Track 9
Track 10

<- Add
Remove ->
Clear All
Reset

Available Tracks:
Intro
Track 2
Track 3
Pretty Fly
Track 5
Track 6
Track 7
Track 8
Track 9
Track 10

Track 02: Track 2   Set Name

OK   Cancel

The track is added at the bottom of the list.

Select a track.

Click to confirm the selection.

Click Remove.

Click to select a track.

Click to clear the list.

To add tracks

1. From the *Available Tracks list*, select the track to be added.
2. Click *Add*.
3. The track is added at the bottom of the list.

To remove tracks

4. In the *Play List*, select the track you wish to remove.
5. Click *Remove*. The track is removed.

To create a new list

6. Click *Clear All* to start from scratch. The *Play List* is cleared entirely.
7. Click *OK* to return to the CD Player and save the list.

The Play List window enables you to programme a choice of tracks to listen to, as you would on the CD Player of your Hi-Fi system. You can skip tracks you do not like or have heard excessively, or loop endlessly on your favourite track. The play list is automatically stored by the CD player, just like the titles you entered for tracks. The next time you listen to the CD, the CD player will play it in the order you imposed. You can clear the list (see Step 6) whenever you wish. The play list is the order in which the list is played. It is managed through four buttons: Add, Remove, Clear All and Reset. Click Reset to return to the basic playing order of the CD, track by track, regardless of the selection you have made.

Checklist

This dialogue box gives access to the two main options for the CD Player.

1 If you have several CD drives or a CD loader, you can select the CD drive used to listen to audio CDs. This is usually drive D:.

2 Independently of any other output volume control, move the sliding cursor to increase or decrease the audio output volume for the CD drive. Maximum output volume is recommended, all the more so as you have tools to decrease the volume at another level (Volume Control).

3 Click OK to confirm the changes and return to the Control Panel.

Select active CD Player

Control Panel/Multimedia/CD Music

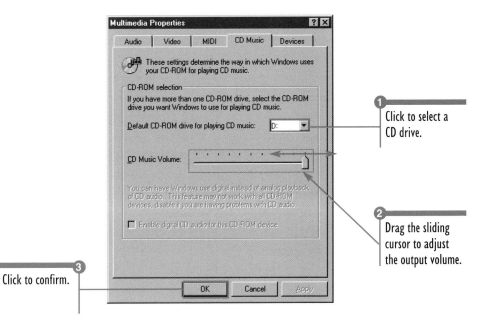

Click to select a CD drive.

Drag the sliding cursor to adjust the output volume.

Click to confirm.

In some cases, the sounds transmitted by a CD Player are of horrendous quality. The speakers crackle, the sound is deafening, the treble far too light. How can you solve the problem? You must first locate it. The two most common causes are: the speakers are not properly connected to the sound card, or there is a bad connection between the CD Player and the sound card. The first case is easy to deal with: make sure that the connectors of the speakers are properly plugged into the 'spk out' port and not into the 'line out' port (a port that can be used to connect a tape recorder, for example). In the second case you will have to 'get under the bonnet'. The CD Player and the sound card must be connected directly by means of a cable. Make sure that they are and read through the documentation of the CD Player and the sound card to find out which connectors to use on the two ends of the cable.

Sound card controls
Start / Programs / SoundBlaster AWE64

The SoundBlaster card is supplied with an impressive set of programs that form a mini recording studio. Some of these programs replicate programs we have already seen, such as the sound mixer or the CD Player. But the SoundBlaster studio is more complete and performs better than the small applications provided with Windows 95/98. The programs can be divided into categories. Three players can play sounds from audio CDs, from wave files (.wav) and, most importantly, from **MIDI** files (for an introduction to **MIDI**, see page 107). These three players obey the orders of a master remote control device known as Creative Remote. Of course, the software package includes a sound recorder and mixer, whose functions are identical to that of the Windows Volume Control, but with a more attractive presentation. Creative Soundo'LE is a wave recorder, like the Windows Sound Recorder, which it resembles in the way it works. The sophisticated Wavestudio can then be used to edit wave files, using special effects, copying and pasting sequences, etc. For its part, Creative Wave Synth/WG can play any wave, and includes a synthesiser capable of playing several notes and several instruments simultaneously. **MIDI** files will be read by the Creative **MIDI** Instrument Mapper. Finally, AWE32 Control is a toolbox used by the other programs. It includes special effects, sound databases, etc. If you are wondering why all the names begin with 'Creative', it is because the manufacturer of SoundBlaster cards is a company named 'Creative Labs'.

TIP
Why are we only discussing SoundBlaster cards? Good question. Because they have become a de facto standard. Most games, for example, are programmed to be played with a SoundBlaster card. This is true to such an extent, that many other cards now use a SoundBlaster emulator (a built-in program that imitates the way the SoundBlaster card works).

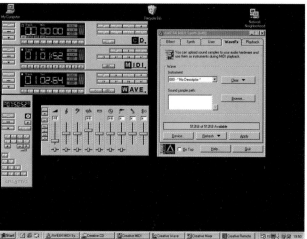

The main difference between the Creative applications that come with the SoundBlaster card and the Windows applications (CD Player, Sound Recorder, etc.) lies in the layout and accessibility of the controls and in the general aspect of the user interface. Each sound source is handled by a dedicated tool: MIDI files by the MIDI player, CD by the CD player, .wav files by the Wave player. All the tools have the same appearance. As illustrated, the three panels can be opened simultaneously.

Your pointer will often be shaped like a hand, when you adjust the volume or you fast forward through a track by clicking the left button.

For information on each command, please refer to the description of the Windows CD Player and its options (pages 83 and 84) or of the Sound Recorder (page 74).

Player controls

Start/Programs/Creative/CTSND/Creative CD

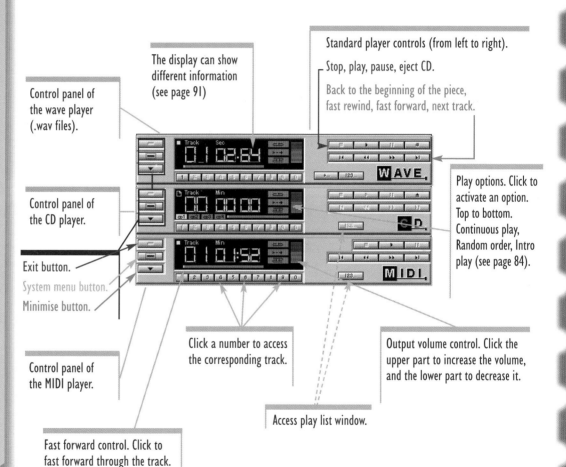

The display can show different information (see page 91)

Control panel of the wave player (.wav files).

Control panel of the CD player.

Exit button.

System menu button.

Minimise button.

Control panel of the MIDI player.

Fast forward control. Click to fast forward through the track.

Click a number to access the corresponding track.

Access play list window.

Standard player controls (from left to right).

Stop, play, pause, eject CD.

Back to the beginning of the piece, fast rewind, fast forward, next track.

Play options. Click to activate an option. Top to bottom. Continuous play, Random order, Intro play (see page 84).

Output volume control. Click the upper part to increase the volume, and the lower part to decrease it.

Edit play list

Button 123, page 89

Click to play the intro-
duction of the track
selected from a list.

Click and enter the
title of the CD.

CD Playlist

The song remains the same (CD1)

	Add	
01 Celebration day	Add	01 Rock and Roll
02 The song remains the same	Add All	02 Celebration day
03 Rain song		03 The song remains the same
04 Dazed and confused	Remove	04 Rain song
05 Track 6		05 Dazed and confused
06 Track 7	Remove All	06 Track 6
07 Track 8		07 Track 7
08 Track 9		08 Track 8
09 Track 10		09 Track 9
10 Track 11		10 Track 10
11 Track 12		11 Track 11

Rain song

Led Zeppelin

Done
Cancel
Help

Click and enter
the name of the
selected track.

Click a track without
name to select it.

Press [Enter] activate
the changes.

Click to confirm
changes.

Click and enter the
name of the artist.

Enter a comment on the
selection if you wish.

You can create a play list as indicated on page 85 in the case of the Windows CD Player.
The Clear All button is labelled here Remove All. The Reset button is replaced by an Add
All button (provided the Remove All has deleted the list first). You can select several tracks
by clicking them one at the time whilst pressing the [Shift] key.

Checklist

1. In the upper text field, enter the title of the CD.

2. In the list on the right, click a track name to select it.

3. The name of the selected track appears in the text field below the list. Click on it and type a new name for the track (in this case, 'Rain song').

4. In the next text box, illustrated with a face, enter the name of the artist.

5. To confirm the changes, press [Enter]. The old track name, in the list on the right, is replaced by the new name. Select the next track you want to rename. Repeat the same procedure.

6. If you want to add a comment, type it in the text box at the bottom.

7. Click Done to confirm the changes.

Disk and track information:
.... display options.......

Track and collection title

Displays the name of the CD (at the top) as well as the title of the track, which scrolls continuously while playing (at the bottom).

Track time

Displays the number of the track (left) and the time elapsed (right).

Track title and order

Displays the name of the track and its position on the CD.

Track and artist name

Displays the name of the artist (at the top) and the title of the track, which scrolls continuously while playing (at the bottom).

To access the display options, click the right button of the mouse when the pointer is in the display area.

Graphics

Displays the front panel of a player with the wave player on top, the CD player at the centre and the MIDI player at the bottom.

SoundBlaster sound mixer

Start/Programs/SoundBlaster AWE64/Creative Mixer

A Display the recording console.

Select the device(s) you want to listen to. If you want to listen to it and the sound being mixed, the speaker symbol must be displayed in green and show a wave.

B Display options, from top to bottom: without LED; in minimum view; customised or extended.

Adjust the balance for each device.

The sliding cursors are scaled. The selected value is displayed as you drag the cursor.

① **Main volume control**

② **Treble control**

③ **Bass control**

④ **Wave output control**

⑤ **MIDI output control**

⑥ **WaveSynth output control**

⑦ **Reverberation control**

⑧ **CD Player output control**

⑨ **Input volume control**

⑩ **Microphone output control**

⑪ **Speaker output control**

The sound mixer provided with the SoundBlaster card is a little more complete and easier to use than the Windows Volume Control. Of course, it features a sliding cursor and a balance cursor for each input device (CD Player, microphone, Wave, Midi, WaveSynth, etc.).

Several additional controls have been included: the echo control, the base control and its alter ego, the treble control. The last two controls depend on the main output volume control (see left).

A Click the Recording Options button to open the recording mixer.

B This button leads to several options: mask LED (the frequency display disappears), minimum view (the general volume sliding cursor and the LED screen are displayed), customised view and extended view (as illustrated).

Checklist

The recording console supplied with the SoundBlaster card can be used to adjust the level for each recording device simultaneously, like the Windows sound recorder (see page 74). It therefore adjusts the recording level of sounds transmitted to Soundo'LE and recorded by the latter, as we shall see in the next pages.

To prepare to record speech using a microphone, with background music, proceed as follows:

① Check that the microphone is properly plugged in. Select the microphone, and set its input level to the maximum.

② Select the CD Player and set the input level at 40%, so that it does not cover the voice.

③ Run a test: play the CD track from the CD Player, and say your text.

④ If the level seems fine, just leave the settings as they are. You must now open the Soundo'LE to record the text against the background music.

Use recording tools

Recording options button, page 92

① Select the microphone and set the cursor at 100%.

③ Test it. The output sound is displayed on the LED display.

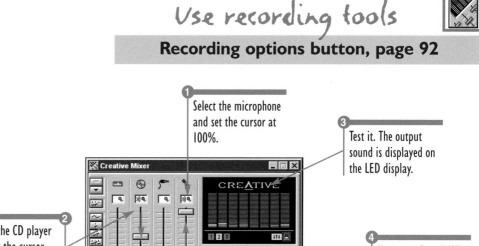

② Select the CD player and set the cursor at 40%.

④ Now open Soundo'LE to record the mix.

The LED screen can display several characteristics of a sound signal. To switch from one to the other, click the LED display.

First, the frequency spectrum. Each band corresponds to a frequency band: 0–155 kHz (very low); 155–310 kHz (low); 310–625 kHz; 625–1250 kHz; 1.25–2.5 kHz; 2.5–5 kHz; 5–10 kHz (high); 10–20 kHz (very high), from left to right.

Second, the balance. This screen displays the level of the signals of the left and right channels. Do not forget that stereo sounds do not display the same level on the left and on the right channel.

Third, the amplitude of the sound wave in relation to the length of the signals. You can edit a similar wave with Wave Editor.

CHAPTER 2 : SOUND

93

Main remote control and its functions

Window control buttons:
Exit, main menu and minimise.

Select player button. Click the button to open a toolbar with three other buttons, then click a button in order to access the corresponding player.

Remote is the generic remote control of the Creative players. It controls the CD player, the Wave player and the MIDI player.

It features standard buttons just like a Hi-Fi system remote control. They have been described and explained in the preceeding pages (pp. 85 ff.).

You do not need to display the player to access its control buttons: use the remote control instead!

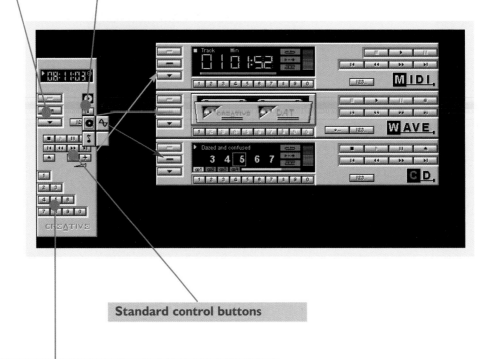

Standard control buttons

Track selection button:
Click a number to play the corresponding track.

Checklist

To record a sound

1. Click *File/New* to create a new blank audio file.

2. Click the recording button as soon as you are ready to play the sounds to be recorded (you have already adjusted the settings in the recording console). Soundo'LE starts recording.

3. When the piece is finished, click the stop button. To do things properly, let the recording run a few more seconds.

4. When the recording is completed, do not forget to save the file using the *File/Save* command.

Recording with Soundo'LE

Start/Programs/Soundblaster AWE64/Soundo'LE

Click File/Save. ④

Click File/New. ①

Recording levels (see page 81).

This box displays the length of the piece.

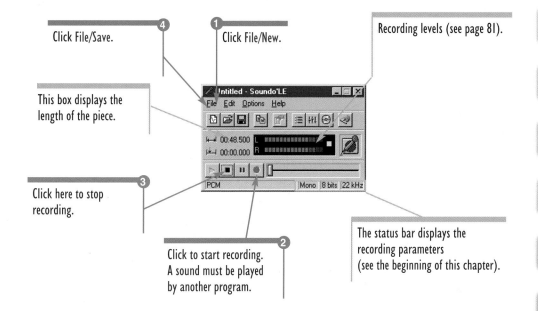

Click here to stop recording. ③

Click to start recording. A sound must be played by another program. ②

The status bar displays the recording parameters (see the beginning of this chapter).

The Soundo'LE program is similar to the Windows Sound Recorder, but more advanced, as it gives access to Wave Studio (see next section). Soundo'LE receives the sound at the output of the recording console without changing the values set in that console. It saves the sound as a .wav file.

Soundo'LE recording flow chart

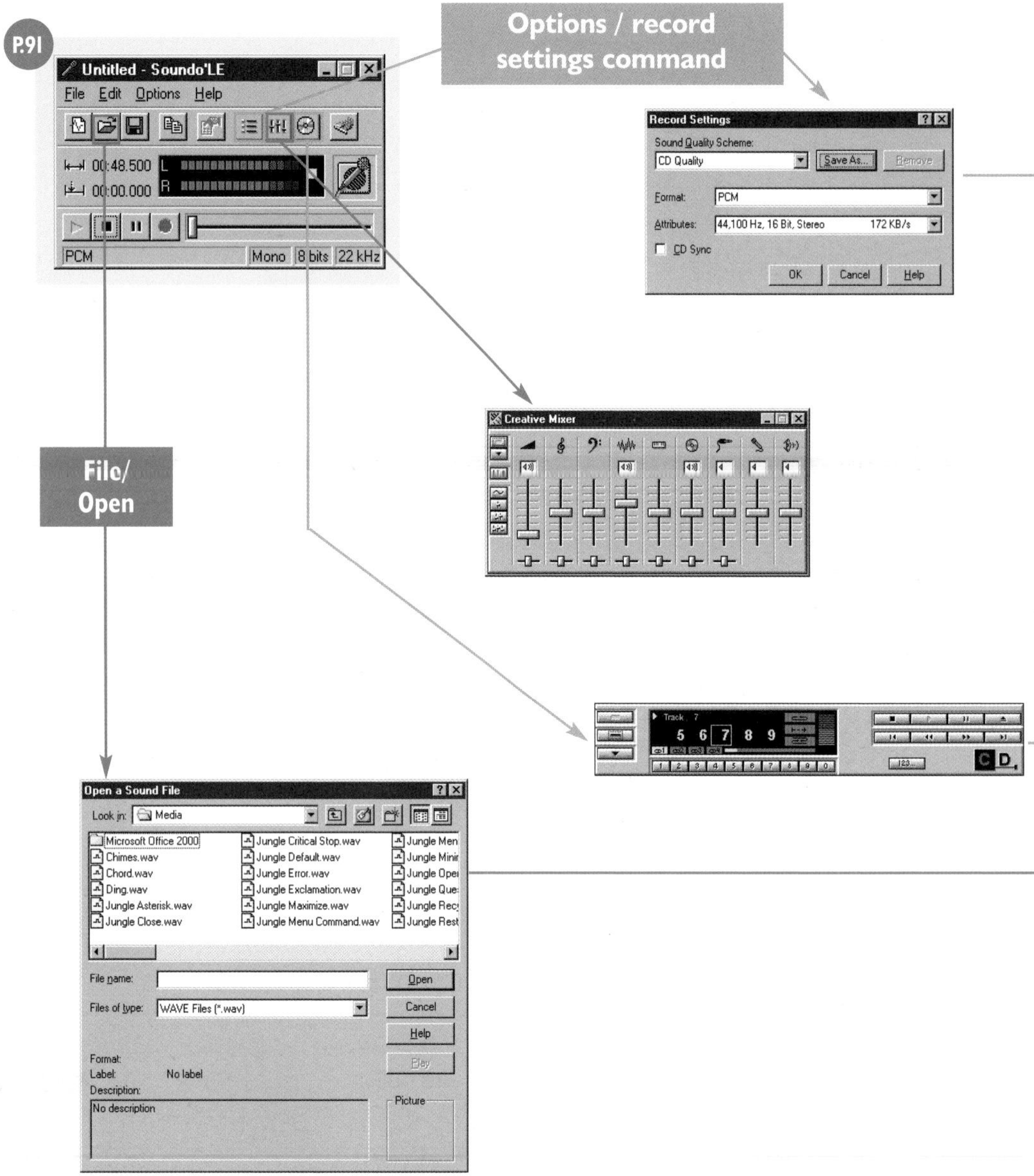

Options / record settings command

P.91

File/ Open

Used to change the current record settings.

Displays the sound Mixer or Recorder.

Displays the CD Player.

Displays an *Open File* dialog box. Select a sound for Soundo'LE to play.

Editing an audio file

The Creative Labs software package includes a wave editing program, or if you prefer, a *.wav* files editing program. You can therefore have fun modifying sounds and mixes recorded with Soundo'LE. In Wave Studio, a *.wav file* is visualised as a wave characterised by its duration, its amplitude (the 'peaks'), and the wavelength (their frequency). You will therefore have to get used to this representation, which is the simplest if you want to isolate a sound or an effect, and have fun duplicating it within the recording or pasting it into another file. Wave Studio can open several audio files simultaneously and lets you switch easily between files.

Wave Studio also offers interesting special effects that you can apply to customise a recorded piece.

TIP
If you want to mix sounds, make sure they were recorded with the same settings. An 8-bit sound cannot be merged properly into a file recorded in 16 bits, and vice versa. However, it is always possible to change the settings of one of the files so that they match.

Select a wave excerpt

Edit/Select all

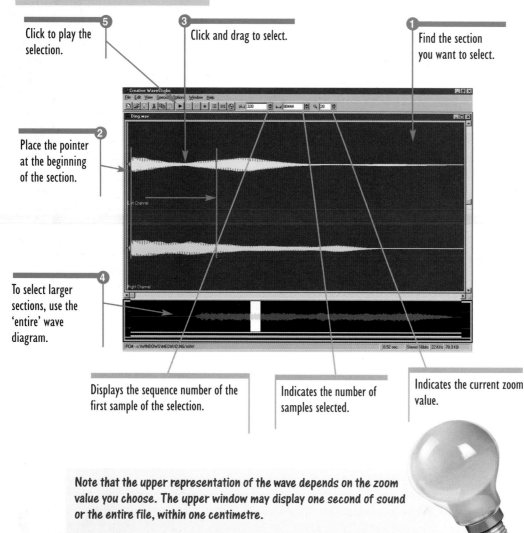

⑤ Click to play the selection.

③ Click and drag to select.

① Find the section you want to select.

② Place the pointer at the beginning of the section.

④ To select larger sections, use the 'entire' wave diagram.

Displays the sequence number of the first sample of the selection.

Indicates the number of samples selected.

Indicates the current zoom value.

Note that the upper representation of the wave depends on the zoom value you choose. The upper window may display one second of sound or the entire file, within one centimetre.

Checklist

① In the wave, find the section you want to select.

② Place the mouse pointer at the beginning of this section and click to start the selection.

③ Drag to the end of the section you want to select.

④ To select a larger section, use the wave at the bottom of the window.

⑤ To play the selection, click the start button.

• • • • • • • • • **Note** • • • • • • • •

To edit a sound you must first select a section of the wave.

Checklist

1. Enter the magnitude of the echo. The magnitude is the power of the echo, expressed in % (from 0% to 100%). The higher the percentage, the more important the echo.

2. Choose the time delay of the echo. Avoid values close to one second: the ear perceives the echo as a fully fledged sound and tries to decipher it, to the detriment of the original, which continues to run.

3. If the file is stereo, select the channel you want the echo to be applied to: Left, Right, or Both.

4. Click OK to apply the echo. In the Wave Studio window, listen to the echo.

••••• **Note** •••••

You can apply a new echo on a file with echo, and thus superpose echo waves until you obtain a metallic sound.

Adding echo to a wave

Special/Add echo

1 Enter the magnitude of the echo. Do some tests. A magnitude of 50% is a good level to start with.

4 Click to confirm.

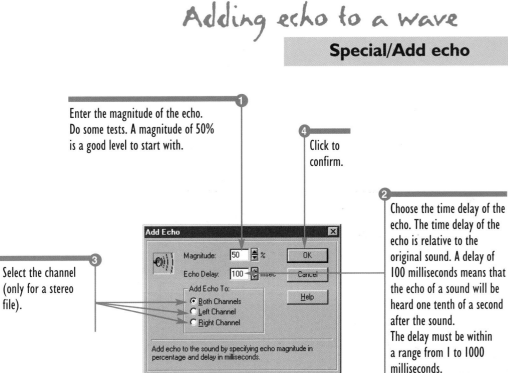

3 Select the channel (only for a stereo file).

2 Choose the time delay of the echo. The time delay of the echo is relative to the original sound. A delay of 100 milliseconds means that the echo of a sound will be heard one tenth of a second after the sound. The delay must be within a range from 1 to 1000 milliseconds.

You have undoubtedly noticed that the representation of the sound (see page 101) has changed from the earlier pages: there are now two waves. The reason for this is that page 93 shows a mono recording while the sound illustrated on page 98 is stereo and, therefore, there are two waves: one for the right speaker (or channel), and the other for the left speaker. Note that all selections are automatically made on the two channels.

Checklist

1. Specify the initial magnitude (see the checklist on the previous page).

2. Select the channel to which the fade-in must be applied (in the case of a stereo file).

3. Click OK to confirm.

Adding a fade-in
Special/Fade-in – Fade-out

The fade-in causes the file to start at the magnitude you selected and increase gradually to the full output volume, which is 100%. If you set a magnitude of 0%, the fade-in will range from silence (0%) to 100%. In a fade-out, the intensity of the sound is diminished gradually, from 100% to the selected magnitude value.

Fade In dialog:

Magnitude: 0 %

Fade In:
- Both Channels
- Left Channel
- Right Channel

OK
Cancel
Help

Fade in the wave data by specifying the starting magnitude in percentage.

Reverse audio file

Special/Reverse – Reverse audio file

These commands are used to reverse a sound i.e. to play it backwards. This reversal can be applied either to the entire file (Reverse file command), or to a selection (Reverse command). In this case, of course, you must have previously selected a section of the wave!

Reverse dialog:

Reverse Playback:
- Both Channels
- Left Channel
- Right Channel

OK
Cancel
Help

Reverse the playback of the wave data for the selected channel(s).

Checklist

1. Select a section of the wave in the Wave Studio window.

2. Click the command.

3. Specify the channel to which the reversal must be applied (in the case of a stereo file).

4. Click OK to confirm.

100

Silence control

Special/Force to silence

A silence, as its name indicates, is a soundless section inserted in a sound file as a pause. The selected section is then replaced by the silence. To insert the silence, select the channel (Right, Left, or Both), use the command presented here.

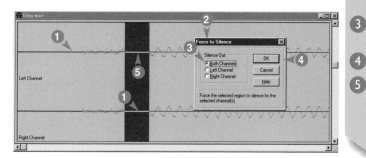

Checklist

1. Select the sound section (or region) to be silenced.
2. Click the *Special/Force To Silence* command, which displays a dialogue box.
3. Select the channel to be silenced.
4. Click *OK* to confirm.
5. In the wave, the section is replaced by a silence… a straight line without amplitude or frequency.

Shift phases

Special/Phase shift

Checklist

1. Select a stereo file section.
2. Click the *Phase Shift* command.
3. Select the channel to shift.
4. Select the shifting unit (time or number of samples)
5. Set the shift value.
6. Click *OK*.

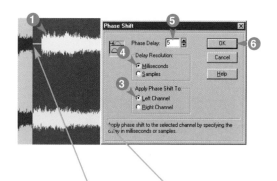

The shift is carried out by inserting at the beginning of the selected channel a silence equivalent to the value selected in (5). This silence is also inserted at the end of the selection in the other channel.

Phase shift

When a stereo music clip is in phase, the left and right channels produce sounds with the same frequency, which vary in the same way. When phase shift occurs, there is a delay (in milliseconds) introduced between the selected channel and the other. If too long, this delay creates an echo effect. This special effect gives the sound more 'volume.'

Checklist

1 Select the number of channels: 1 (mono) or 2 (stereo).

2 Change the sampling rate.

3 Change the coding.

4 Click OK to confirm.

Changing sound settings

Special/Convert format

For more information on the commonly used settings, see page 60. A mono sound can be converted into a stereo equivalent using this dialog box. You do not need to change all settings: you can just change the sampling frequency, for example.

Convert Format

Channels:
- ◯ Mono
- ◉ Stereo 1

OK
Cancel 4
Help

Sampling Rate:
- ◯ 11025 Hz
- ◉ 22050 Hz 2
- ◯ 44100 Hz

Sampling Size:
- ◯ 8 bits
- ◉ 16 bits 3

Select Stereo or Mono, frequency and sample size (8 or 16 bit).

Changing sampling frequency only

Special/Change frequency

Remember, increasing the sampling frequency makes a sound more accurate – but not more harmonic: the program cannot create additional frequencies. When you reduce the frequency, this accuracy is cut drastically, but the change reduces the size of the file considerably.

Modify Frequency

Playback Rate:
- ◯ 11025 Hz
- ◉ 22050 Hz 1
- ◯ 44100 Hz

OK
Cancel 2
Help

Modify the playback rate of the wave by selecting a new frequency.

Checklist

1 Select the new sampling frequency.

2 Click OK to confirm.

Checklist

You can open several waves in *Wave Editor* and go easily from one window to the other – to copy a section of a file and paste it into another file for example.

1. Click *File/Open* to open each of the files.

2. Resize the windows in order to view the different files as clearly as possible.

The *Window* menu contains several commands that enable you to reorganise the program window, and to use the space without wasting time. The screen shot illustrates the *Window/Vertical Tile* command. You can also select *Window/ Horizontal Tile* to arrange the windows horizontally or *Window/ Cascade* to put all windows on top of each other but with enough offset to be able to click any one and make it the active window.

Working with several sound files

Windows Menu

The active document window displays a coloured title bar.

Vertical tiling

Horizontal tiling

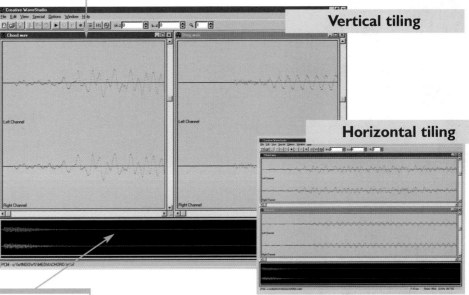

The wave of the selected window is displayed in the lower part of the program window.

If you prefer to open several files and to display them in maximised windows, use the *Window* menu to go from one file to the other. Just click on the file name to bring it to the front and make it the active window.

Copy a section from one file to another

Edit/Copy and Edit/Paste

Copy it. ④

Paste the excerpt. ⑥

Open several files. ①

Resize the windows to optimise the display. ②

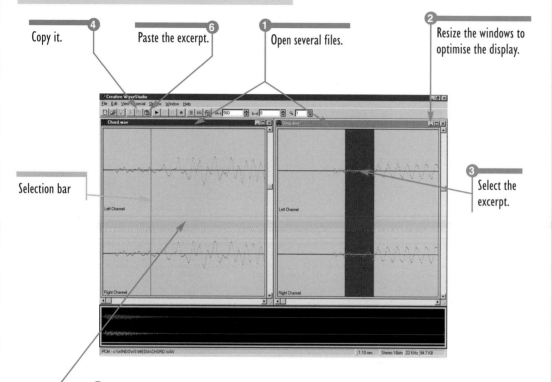

Selection bar

Select the excerpt. ③

Click in the window of the receiving file. ⑤

To simplify the procedure, use the same zoom value in both windows. Also, avoid pasting stereo sound into a mono file. Wave Studio allows this type of insertion, but the result is often disappointing. You can also paste a copy of a section into the same file, at another location. If you want to test your sampler qualities, you may want to repeat a section several times. Select a section and click Special/Repeat! as many times as you wish. A copy of the selected range is inserted to the right of the current selection every time you click the command.

[Ctrl] + [C]
then
[Ctrl] + [V]

Checklist

① Click File/Open for each document you wish to open (we have opened two).

② Resize the windows to view the files side by side. Here, we used the Window/Vertical Tile command.

③ Select the range you want to copy.

④ Click Edit/Copy.

⑤ Click in the window of the file in which you will paste the selection, then click to insert the selection bar at the right place.

⑥ Click Edit/Paste. The range is inserted to the left of the selection bar.

Checklist

1. Click *File/Open* for each file you wish to open.

2. Resize the windows to view the files side by side. Here, we used the *Window/Horizontal Tile* command.

3. Select the excerpt you want to copy.

4. Click *Edit/Copy*.

5. Click in the window of the file in which you will paste the selection, then click to insert the selection bar at the right place.

6. Click *Edit/Paste and Mix*. A dialog box is displayed.

7. Select the type of mix.

8. Click *OK* to confirm the mix.

9. The wave is modified. Now listen to it…

Pasting and mixing an excerpt

Edit/Copy and Edit/Paste and Mix

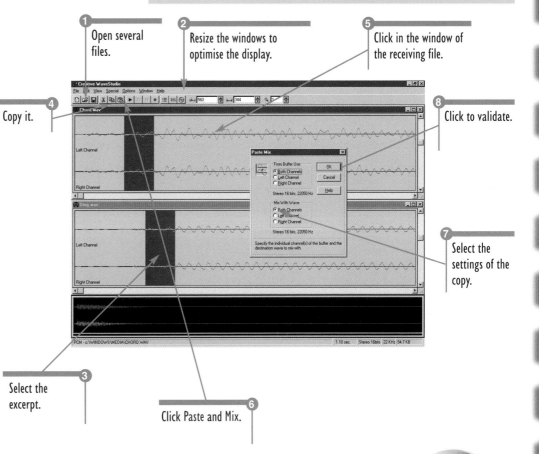

1. Open several files.

2. Resize the windows to optimise the display.

5. Click in the window of the receiving file.

4. Copy it.

8. Click to validate.

7. Select the settings of the copy.

3. Select the excerpt.

6. Click Paste and Mix.

What is the difference between the simple paste and the paste and mix procedure? The first inserts the selection in the sound file by cutting it. The selection is intact and the piece is cut by the latter. In a paste and mix procedure, the excerpt is inserted in the file without cutting it. Instead, the two are blended from the selection bar to the end. It is as if a sound (an instrument, a voice, etc.) has been superposed onto the original sound.

Editing display colours

Options/Display colours

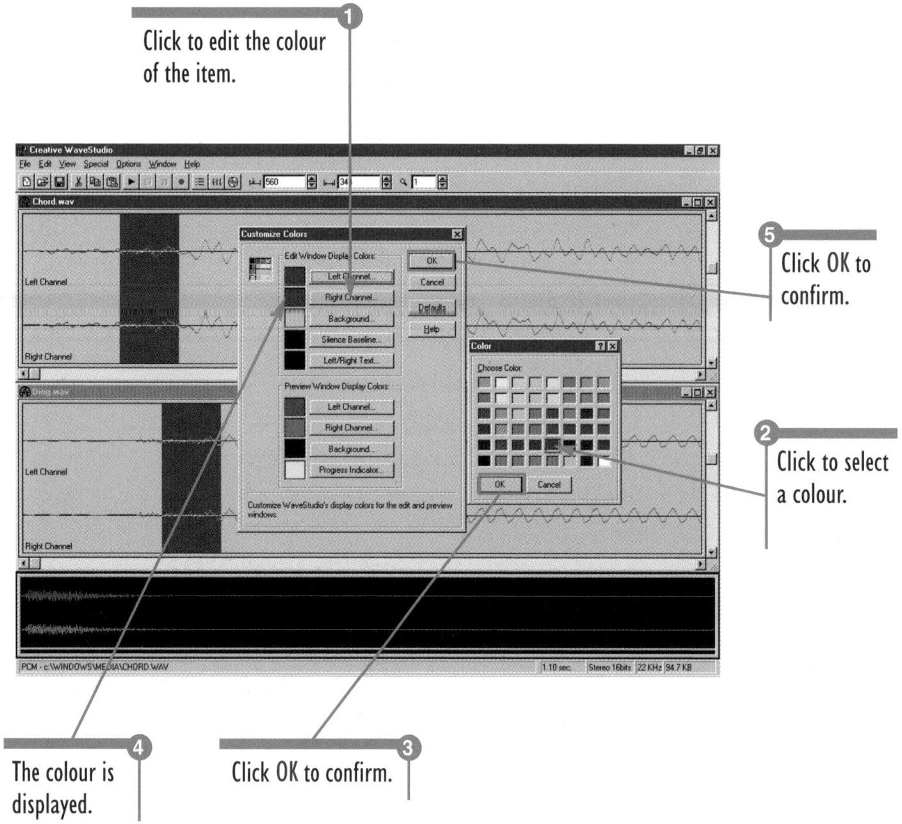

Click to edit the colour
of the item. **①**

⑤ Click OK to
confirm.

② Click to select
a colour.

④ The colour is
displayed.

③ Click OK to confirm.

Checklist

Just for the fun of it, or
to spare your eyes, you
may decide to edit the
colours of the different
areas of the window.
The procedure is simple:

① Click the item whose
colour you want to edit.

② A colour palette opens.
Click the desired colour
to select it.

③ Click OK to confirm.

④ The new colour is
displayed in front of
the item. Repeat the
procedure for any other
items.

⑤ Click OK to confirm the
change of colours.

Introduction to MIDI

MIDI stands for Musical Instrument Digital Interface. It is neither a new kind of synthesiser nor a sophisticated program, but a standard, a set of rules used to communicate musical compositions. The **MIDI** language, which made it possible for software and hardware from different manufacturers to talk to each other, does not use the conventional representation of music with its notes and staves. Instead, it encodes sound, and provides information about the pitch of the sound, its length, and the instrument that must play it. For instance, it will describe how, in a certain piece, a '**C**' note must be played loud, in the second octave, for four seconds, by instrument number 079 (i.e. the ocarina). This is very flexible: change the instrument number, and you can hear the same four-second '**C**' played by an alto saxophone, or a grand piano. Since 1991, each instrument has been attributed a number, which is the same for all machines, and all programs. The key instrument in the **MIDI** universe is still the synthesiser so beloved by Vangelis or Jean-Michel Jarre. It is used to compose and directly encode music. The SoundBlaster is supplied with a virtual synthesiser ('virtual' because it is a program). You can thus compose small pieces, record them (in *.wav* format, thanks to Soundo'LE) and edit them (with Wave Studio), etc. To achieve this, you must identify the **MIDI** device connected to your computer, specify the **MIDI** settings... and play on the keyboard, using the mouse.

Many effects can be set with precision.

TIP
Several MIDI files of considerable size were supplied with your SoundBlaster card. They were copied onto your hard disk, in the Media folder. You can play these files with the MIDI player described on pages 88 and 89. Many CDs supplied with computer magazines contain MIDI files too (extension : *.mid*).

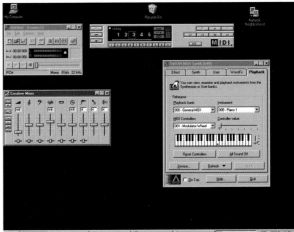

Setting up a MIDI device

Start/Programs/SoundBlaster AWE64/ Creative MIDI Instrument Mapper

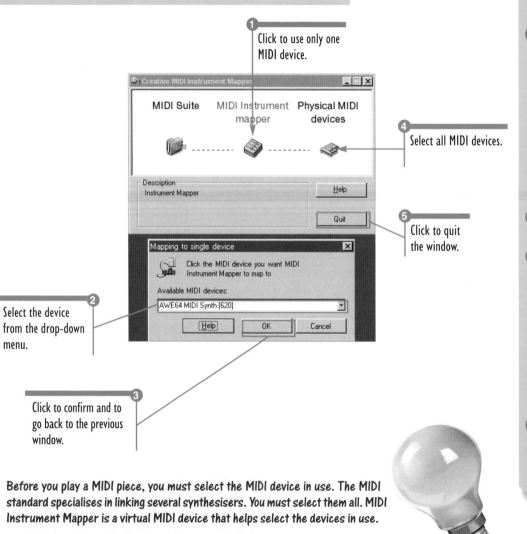

Click to use only one MIDI device.

MIDI Suite **MIDI Instrument mapper** **Physical MIDI devices**

Select all MIDI devices.

Description
Instrument Mapper

Help

Quit

Click to quit the window.

Mapping to single device

Click the MIDI device you want MIDI Instrument Mapper to map to

Available MIDI devices:

AWE64 MIDI Synth [620]

Help   OK   Cancel

Select the device from the drop-down menu.

Click to confirm and to go back to the previous window.

Before you play a MIDI piece, you must select the MIDI device in use. The MIDI standard specialises in linking several synthesisers. You must select them all. MIDI Instrument Mapper is a virtual MIDI device that helps select the devices in use.

Checklist

1. Click here to use only one device for your MIDI applications. If you select this option, you must also select the device.

2. In the list of MIDI devices, select the one you want to use: the synthesiser (AWE64 MIDI Synth), the instrument database (WaveSynth/ WG, whose instruments have a better sound quality than those of the sound card), or the MIDI output to a real synthesiser.

3. Click *OK* to confirm your choice.

4. If you do not wish to be creative at this stage, trust the 'simulators' built in the SoundBlaster card. Click *MIDI Devices*. You will access the complete set described in the preceding point. This choice is strongly recommended for amateurs.

5. Click *Exit*. The program will store your choices in memory.

To play at the keyboard

1. Click a key on the virtual keyboard. If you keep the button down, you lengthen the note. Click another key to change note.

2. To go to a higher scale, click the sliding cursor and drag it up one notch.

To change instrument

3. Click the arrow to open the menu and select another instrument. Click a key to test it.

To add sound effects

4. Click the MIDI control-lers drop-down menu, to access sound effects: echo, chorus, modu-lation, etc. Select the effect you want to apply.

5. Adjust the intensity of the sound effect with the sliding cursor. Values range from 0 to 127.

6. To quit the application, click *Quit*.

Composing a MIDI piece

Start/Programs/SoundBlaster AWE64/ AWE Control/Play tab

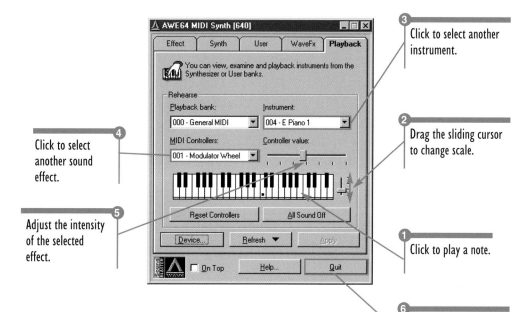

Click to select another instrument.

Drag the sliding cursor to change scale.

Click to play a note.

Click to exit the virtual synthesiser.

Click to select another sound effect.

Adjust the intensity of the selected effect.

Thanks to this virtual keyboard, you can create your own melodies and have fun playing them with different instruments. Numerous sound effects are also available under the heading 'Controllers'. The chorus and echo are among the best known. If you cannot hear what you are playing, make sure the MIDI devices are properly set (see previous page), the speakers are plugged in and switched on, and the MIDI sliding cursor of the sound mixer is correctly set.

CHAPTER 2 : SOUND

MIDI effects

Start/Programs/SoundBlaster AWE64/ AWE Control/Effect tab

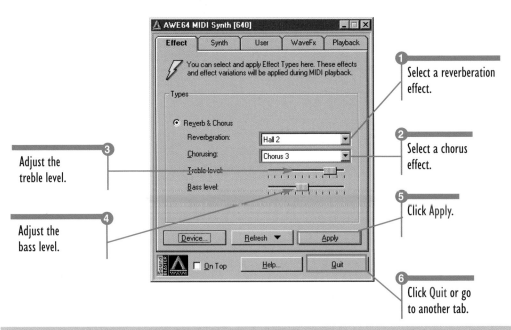

① Select a reverberation effect.

② Select a chorus effect.

③ Adjust the treble level.

④ Adjust the bass level.

⑤ Click Apply.

⑥ Click Quit or go to another tab.

Checklist

This dialogue box is used to adjust the two main effects, as well as treble and bass levels of your MIDI compositions.

① Select a type of reverberation. This effect will be applied to all keys of the virtual keyboard.

② Select a type of chorus. This effect will also be applied to all keys.

③ Adjust the treble level.

④ Adjust the bass level.

⑤ Click Apply and then the Playback tab to play at the keyboard.

⑥ Click Quit to exit the AWE64 synthesiser.

••••• **Warning** •••••

As long as you have not clicked Apply, the effects will not be taken into account, and you will hear no difference when you play the notes.

List of effects

Reverberation (Effect tab)
This is the natural echo of a concert hall. There are eight types of resonance in the drop-down menu.

Chorusing (Effect tab)
This is a virtual chorus which lavishes synthesised sound with warmth and depth. Eight types of chorus are available.

Stunt pedal (Playback tab)
Support pedal. Boosts the quality of the sound. A key will continue to play the corresponding note even if you click a new key. The sound will continue playing for as long as the key is pressed.

Modulator (Playback tab)
Adjusts the frequency of the note played, adding harmonics.

CHAPTER 2 : SOUND

Start/Programs/Soundblaster AWE64/Soundo'LE

Checklist

Remember, the Soundo'LE program generates only *.wav* files. This means that you can edit your melody with Wave Studio, but, you will not be able to play it with another instrument afterwards.

To record a melody

1 Click *File/New* to create a new blank audio file.

2 Adjust the MIDI settings in the recording console. Then, click the recording button as soon as you are ready to click on the keys of the keyboard to compose the melody. Soundo'LE starts recording. The dials display the length of the recording.

3 At the end of your melody, click the stop button.

4 Do not forget to save the file with the command *File/Save*.

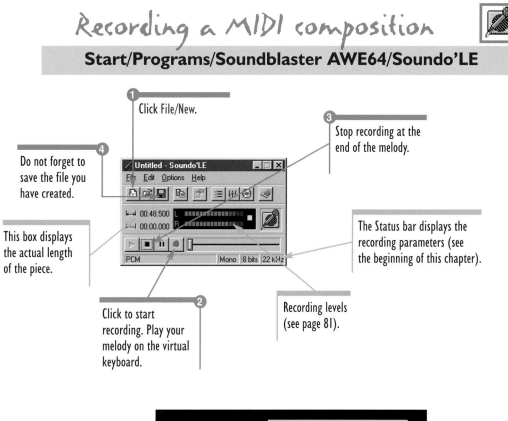

① Click File/New.

④ Do not forget to save the file you have created.

③ Stop recording at the end of the melody.

This box displays the actual length of the piece.

The Status bar displays the recording parameters (see the beginning of this chapter).

② Click to start recording. Play your melody on the virtual keyboard.

Recording levels (see page 81).

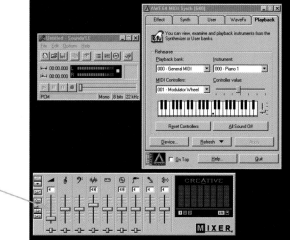

Do not forget to specify the recording level of MIDI sounds in the Sound Recorder.

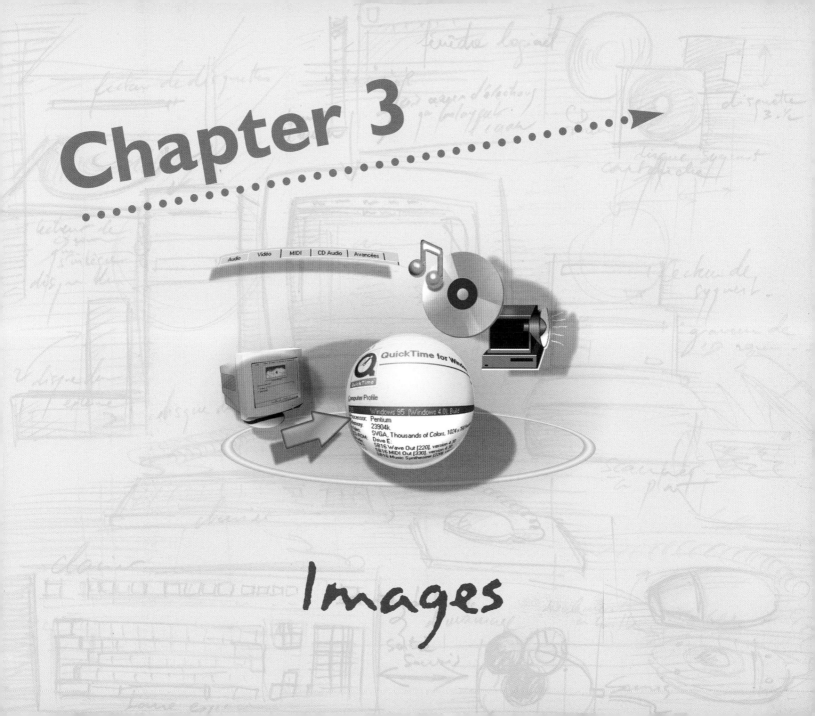

Chapter 3

Images

Characteristics of digital images

Regardless of its source, an image that is to be entered into a computer system, either to be displayed or to be edited, must always be digitised, i.e. encoded into strings of '0's and '1's. Digital images have specific characteristics, such as their colour mode, their resolution, the format under which they are saved and their size. Depending on what you intend to do with an image (four-colour printing, photography, newspaper or web publication) you will adjust its colours using one scale or another. The resolution of an image determines its precision and, therefore, its clarity. Once again, think of what the image will be used for: will it be printed as a full **A4** page, or the size of a postage stamp? The third basic characteristic of an image is the format chosen to manipulate it and to store it.

Just as the format of a sound file influences the size of the file, the format of a picture greatly influences the size of the file once it is saved. Here again, the final destination of the image will influence the choice of the format: the Internet requires small files such as .GIFs or .JPEGs, while four-colour printing requires denser images such as .TIFFs which consume more memory. The last characteristic of the image is its size, which dictates, to a certain extend, what you can do with it: you would not, for instance, use a 4 x 5 cm image as a cover for a magazine.

HOW TO

If you are not sure yet about the destination of an image, and the capacity of your hard disk or of your storage device allows for it, select the most precise format, the highest resolution and the largest possible size. You can always lower these values afterwards.

Selecting the right image format

To save an image you must give it a format. It is simple: an image without a format does not exist. The format is usually indicated by the file name extension. The file name extension therefore provides information about the type of the image, its coding, or origin: the **CDR** format, for example, indicates that the image is in a **CorelDRAW** format. The format of an image influences the space it will occupy on a hard disk, how the image could be used, and also the program that must be used to edit the image. There is usually a data compression method adapted to each image format, in order to reduce the size of the files (a subject we will discuss on page 118). There are also bitmap formats and vector formats. In bitmap formats the image is saved in the form of a grid composed of thousands of dots. Each dot is defined, which makes such images difficult to edit and retouch. If you attempt to enlarge them, for example, new dots are created. You just have to hope the program will give the new dots the appropriate colour! Vector formats, on the other hand, translate the elements of the image (curves, straight lines, etc.) into vectors. There is no quality loss when enlarging. Today most programs for the PC and the Macintosh can read most formats.

TIP

If you wish to print images, bear in mind that most print shops use machines that are fully Macintosh compatible but incompatible with PCs. You can do one of two things: either transfer the items from your PC to a Macintosh, and make the final copy of the ready-to-print job, or try to ensure maximum PC–Mac compatibility. Use formats that can be read by both platforms.

Extension	Format	Source	Platform	Type	Use
BMP	Windows Bitmap	Windows	PC	bitmap	internal in PC
EPS	Encapsulated PostScript	page description for laser printers	mixed	vector	Desktop Publishing (DTP)
GIF	Graphic Interchange Format	CompuServe	mixed	bitmap	Internet
JPEG	Joint Photograph Experts Group	digital photography standard	mixed	bitmap	Internet
Photoshop	Photoshop	native format of the program	mixed	bitmap	DTP
PICT	Picture	Format	Macintosh format	bitmap	Internal in Macintosh
PNG	Portable Network Graphics	Internet	mixed	bitmap	Internet
TIFF	Tagged Image File Format	standard format	mixed	bitmap	DTP, data transfer

Examples of image formats

Model image

Photoshop images

Used extensively in Desktop Publishing to store a maximum of information about the image, or to store independent layers. To exchange images with other programs (insert an image in QuarkXpress, for instance), you must convert the image to **TIFF** format. Size of the original image in **PSD** (Photoshop 2.5) : 1046 kb – more than one Mb.

BMP images (bitmap)

Created by Microsoft for use in Windows, the BMP format is shunned by professionals because of its very poor image restoration quality and the difficulties it creates (the images are bitmaps). Size of original image in **BMP**: 1153 kb – more than one Mb.

JPEG images

Used extensively on the Internet, where their small size increases the transmission speed over telephone lines. **JPEG** uses a powerful, sophisticated compression algorithm. Size of original image in **JPEG**: 78 kb.

TIFF images

Used extensively in DTP and in printing. Excellent quality but discouraging size. LZW compression. Size of original image in **TIFF** format: 874 kb – nearly one Mb.

GIF images

Created by CompuServe, the **GIF** format is used by Web page designers because of the small size of the bitmap images it generates. Its high compression does not compromise the quality of the images: Size of original image in **GIF**: 225 kb.

Data compression

Today, the size of the image used on the cover page of a magazine can easily reach 100 Mb. Imagine that you prepare three versions of that cover, that you keep each stage of the work and that you have a six-month contract. How many disks will you need to buy? Data compression was created to spare a graphic artist the trouble of having to deal with such situations on a daily basis. The principle is simple: reduce the size of the files. The method commonly applied looks for repetitive patterns and encodes only once a sequence that, for example, is repeated three times in the image. Of course, it keeps track of the location of the three sequences in the image, using conventional Cartesian co-ordinates.

Compression helps transmit images more rapidly, especially if they have to go through the telephone network when sent via the Internet. Note that it is not only images that are compressed: sound, video, text and even programs can be compressed to take up less space. The compression champion in the PC universe is **WinZip**. We will devote a few pages to it in chapter five.

HOW TO

How does software compress an image? It will first draw up a list of colours, and attribute a number to each colour (1 for purple, 2 for light blue, etc.). It will then give the corresponding number to the colour of each dot. Finally, it will draw up a new map of the image. If five purple squares are found in a row, it will retain 5, etc.

Not compressed

1	1	2	2	4	4	3	3
3	1	4	4	1	1	3	3
1	2	2	2	1	1	1	2
1	4	4	4	3	3	1	1
1	2	1	1	1	4	4	1
1	3	3	2	2	2	2	2
1	4	4	1	3	3	3	3

← WinUnzip, etc.

WinZip, etc. →

Compressed

2 (1)	2(2)	2(4)	2(3)	
1(3)	1(1)	2(4)	2(1)	2(3)
1(1)	3(2)	3(1)	1(2)	
1(1)	3(4)	2(3)	2(1)	
1(1)	1(2)	3(1)	2(4)	1(1)
1(1)	2(3)	5(2)		
1(1)	2(4)	1(1)	4(3)	

Resolution

Some resolutions	
PC screen:	96 dpi
Low quality image:	50 dpi
Average quality image:	100–150 dpi
Good quality image:	250–300 dpi
Laserjet printer:	600–1200 dpi
Flat scanner:	2400 dpi
Linotronic photosetter:	2500 dpi

The resolution of an image influences its graphic quality, clarity and purity. A high-resolution image could be placed on the cover of a magazine without any grains other than those left by the printing press and the grain screen specific to the paper used. Conversely, a low resolution image will at times not even make it onto the Internet!

The resolution of an image is measured in dots per inch (dpi). This unit indicates the number of pixels (picture elements) distributed over a distance of one inch (i.e. 2.54 cm). To be used in printing, an image must have a minimum resolution of 250 dpi. To be used on a Web page, on the other hand, it should not exceed 96 dpi (the resolution of the best screens), since the image will be used on screen and is not meant to be printed. The resolution and the size of an image are inextricably linked, as we shall see on the next page.

HOW TO

You will note the highly visible 'stair stepping' effect on the 30 dpi photograph. It is called pixellisation because pixels (picture elements) become visible!

TIP

Always use images of the highest resolution possible, even if they need to be reduced to be brought in line with the intended use. If you keep the high definition original on the hard disk, you will not risk having one day to create high resolution images from lower quality ones (such as, for example, an image whose resolution you have lowered; see box on the next page for more details).

Image at 30 dpi

A 300 dpi image

Change image resolution

Image/Image size (in Photoshop)

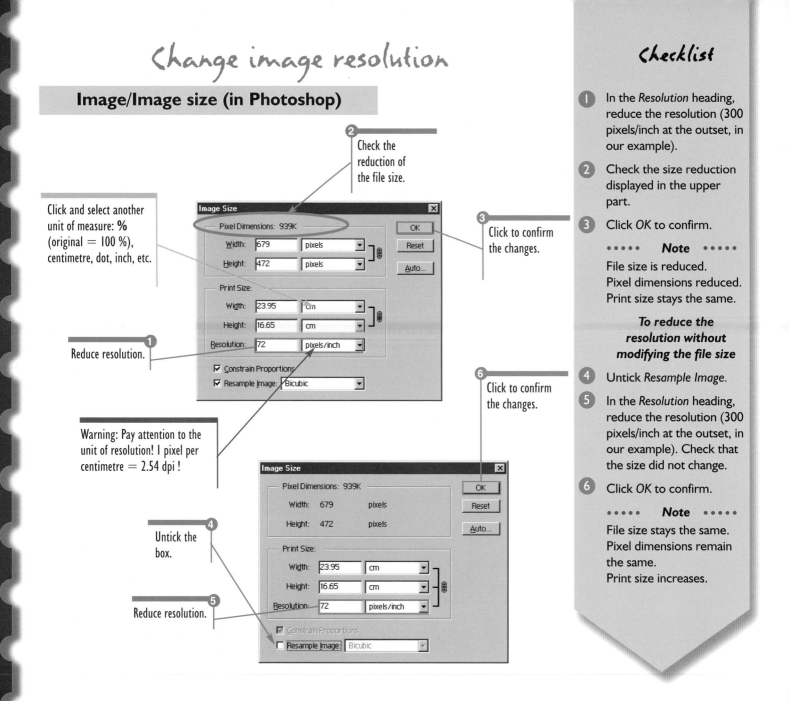

Check the
reduction of
the file size.

Click and select another
unit of measure: %
(original = 100 %),
centimetre, dot, inch, etc.

Image Size

Pixel Dimensions: 939K

Width: 679 pixels

Height: 472 pixels

OK
Reset
Auto...

Print Size:

Width: 23.95 cm

Height: 16.65 cm

Resolution: 72 pixels/inch

☑ Constrain Proportions
☑ Resample Image: Bicubic

Reduce resolution.

Click to confirm
the changes.

Warning: Pay attention to the
unit of resolution! 1 pixel per
centimetre = 2.54 dpi !

Click to confirm
the changes.

Image Size

Pixel Dimensions: 939K

Width: 679 pixels

Height: 472 pixels

OK
Reset
Auto...

Print Size:

Width: 23.95 cm

Height: 16.65 cm

Resolution: 72 pixels/inch

☑ Constrain Proportions
☐ Resample Image: Bicubic

Untick the
box.

Reduce resolution.

Checklist

1. In the *Resolution* heading, reduce the resolution (300 pixels/inch at the outset, in our example).

2. Check the size reduction displayed in the upper part.

3. Click *OK* to confirm.

••••• **Note** •••••
File size is reduced.
Pixel dimensions reduced.
Print size stays the same.

To reduce the resolution without modifying the file size

4. Untick *Resample Image*.

5. In the *Resolution* heading, reduce the resolution (300 pixels/inch at the outset, in our example). Check that the size did not change.

6. Click *OK* to confirm.

••••• **Note** •••••
File size stays the same.
Pixel dimensions remain the same.
Print size increases.

Examples of different resolutions for the same image

Original
Width: **768 pixels**
Length: **512 pixels**
Number of colours: **millions**
Resolution: **300 pixels/inch**

When you resample the image to reduce its size in line with the reduction of the resolution for example, you ask Photoshop to recalculate an image on the basis of the new resolution. During this process, Photoshop deletes the superfluous pixels. When the resolution goes down from 300 to 100 pixels/inch, the image is nine times less precise. This means that where there were initially nine pixels, there is now only one, and the program simply needs to choose the basic colour of nine pixels. The problem is that it is impossible to increase the resolution afterwards. How would you expect Photoshop to recreate nine pixels from a single one?

Preparation for the Internet

Change the resolution and resample. The appropriate resolution, for the Internet, is 72 pixels/inch. Note that the image is automatically reduced to its actual size on the screen.

Resize the image

To obtain an image 10 centimetres wide (let us suppose it has to fit in a frame), you have two main options. Either you reframe this image (more about this in the following pages), or you change its print size. Use the dialogue box below. In the width field, enter the appropriate width (10 cm). Make sure that the *Resample Image* option is ticked, and click *OK* to confirm. Once again, this method works well when reducing an image. To maintain image quality, avoid enlarging an image by more than 10%.

Colour modes

Depending on your objective, you can use one of several colour ranges, the best known of which are **RGB** (red–green–blue), **CMYK** (cyan–magenta–yellow–black), **HLS** (hue-lightness-saturation), and Pantone. Note that all devices dealing with images use the **RGB** scale, except for the colour printer (which uses the **CMYK** scale).

Most of these scales are based on a synthetic model of colours. From three or four colours you can recompose all the colours of the spectrum. Used in photography, the **RGB** mode uses an additive colour mixing: mix 100% red with 100% green to obtain yellow. The only problem is that this model produces millions of colours, more than the printer can print. So you must convert colours to print, and thus lose the most brilliant hues.

Used in printing, the **CMYK** model is based on a colour subtraction model (every object illuminated by the sun absorbs – or subtracts – a range of light, and reflects only part of the spectrum (its 'visible' colour). By superposing four layers of basic colours on transparent paper, you can recompose the entire spectrum and print the colours on any paper. The printing industry uses this technique for four-colour printing (for the printing of colour books, magazines, etc.).

For black and white printing, you can choose between a grey scale (up to 256 levels, which makes it possible to retain a high precision of details), or a simple bitmap, in which all pixels are either black or white, without nuance.

Checklist

1 Open the image.

2 Click *Image/Mode/Color mode*.

3 Select the mode you want to use.

••••• **Note** •••••

Do not forget to save the file in order to update the new mode. If you intend to print, work until the last moment in RGB and then convert the image to CMYK right before printing. The RGB mode is richer, so you will see the brightest colours of the image fade. This is normal. Bear in mind, however, that you will never recover these colours again if you switch back from CMYK to RGB. It is a good idea to make a copy of the image before converting it.

Changing the colour range of an image

Image/Mode/Color mode

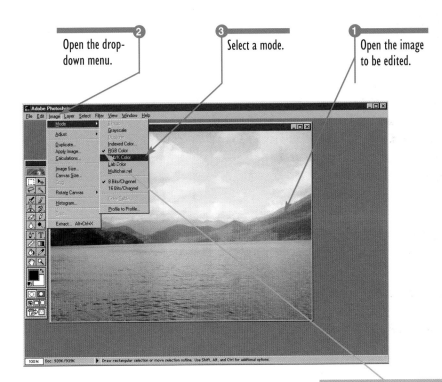

2 Open the drop-down menu.

3 Select a mode.

1 Open the image to be edited.

The current scale of the image is preceded by the symbol ✔.

Paint Shop Pro does not recognise as many different colours as Photoshop. It is limited to the RGB mode, the grey scale, and the HLS (hue – lightness – saturation) modes, as well as CMYK. HLS can reproduce any colour from these three characteristics. The hue is the pure colour, the basis for any colour, measured on a 360° circle (red at 0, yellow at 60, green at 120, cyan at 180, blue at 240 and magenta at 300). The lightness is the intensity of the colour, from black (0%) to saturated (100%) going through all shades from dark to light. Finally, the saturation represents the purity of the colour. The more saturated the colour, the purer it is.

Checklist

It is easy to connect a digital camera to a PC. The camera is usually supplied with a cable that will attach the camera to the serial port of the PC.

To open the photos in an image retouching program

1. Click *File/Import/Digital Camera*. The camera window is displayed.

2. Wait for the camera to transfer all the photographs contained in its memory. They are then displayed as 'thumbnails'. The length of this procedure depends on the number of pictures stored and on their resolution.

3. Click a picture to select it.

4. Give the picture a name.

Importing images from a digital camera

1. Click the File/Import/Digital Camera. The window appears.

File/Import/Digital Camera

To select several images to transfer simultaneously, click on each of them while keeping the [Ctrl] key pressed.

3. Click a photograph to select it.

2. Wait for the program to load the photos.

4. Give it a name.

Here, we used Paint Shop Pro, but we could have also used Photoshop or Picture it ! All recent image retouching programs are compatible with the photo compression format used by cameras (usually JPEG) and the connection to the camera is detected automatically by the software. You can disconnect momentarily the device connected to the serial port, then reconnect it as soon as the photos have been transferred.

Click to delete the selected images.

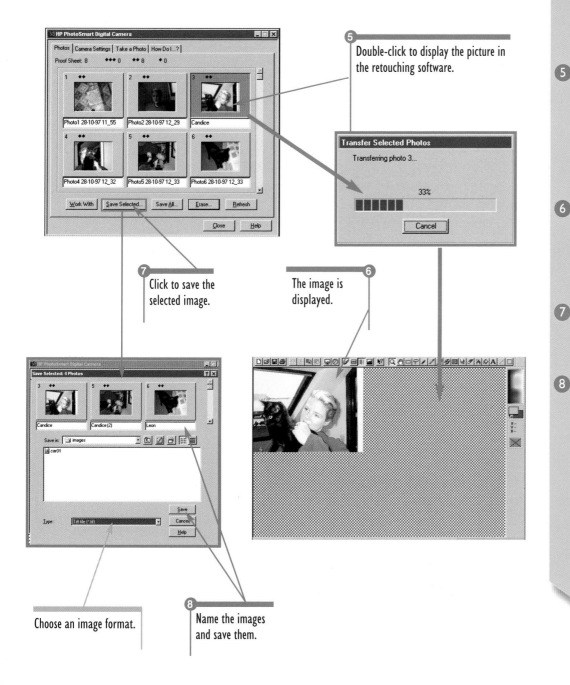

Double-click to display the picture in the retouching software.

⑦ Click to save the selected image.

⑥ The image is displayed.

Choose an image format.

⑧ Name the images and save them.

⑤ Double-click the picture (or click the 'Work with' button) to transfer it to Paint Shop Pro, or to the program you are using. Wait for the transfer to be completed.

⑥ The image is displayed in the retouching program. It doesn't have a name yet. The picture selector has disappeared.

⑦ To save an image directly to the hard disk, select it then click 'Save selected'.

⑧ A File Save window is open. Name each selected photograph (upper part), select a folder and choose the format. To retouch these images, you will have to open them with the File/Open command in the image retouching program.

CHAPTER 3 : IMAGES

125

Image editing tools

View/Tool Palette

There are four groups of tools for editing images. Selection tools are used to select regions of the photograph. We shall have a look at them in the following pages. There are tools to navigate through the image, to enlarge one area, and to move the entire image in its window. There are make-up tools, which are image editing tools. They are used to delete part of the image, create artistic blurs, make the image clear, reduce (virtually) the exposure time, and carry out other such manipulations. Finally, the drawing tools are used to draw geometric forms and lines in an image, and to colour selected areas.

HOW TO

Left: tool palette of Adobe Photoshop 5. Right: tool palette of Paint Shop Pro 4.14. Note the similarity.

Rectangular marquee tool

This is the first of several selection tools, and one of the most precise. You can set its form (ellipse, row, column) and size (down to a pixel in height and width). This is the first tool you will use to select.

Click in the upper left corner of the area you want to select, then drag the marquee whilst keeping the button of the mouse pressed.

Magic wand tool

The magic wand selects according to lightness and colour criteria. Point the wand at a pixel and click; the wand selects all adjacent points with the same lightness. Click another point (of different lightness) and the selection is altogether different. Naturally, you can change the selection area by changing the tolerance value. If you increase this value, you will select a larger area of the image.

In our example, all you have to do is click in the blue-tinted area, on either side of the elephant's trunk, to select the entire area. You could then, for example, place a white background there.

Lasso tool

A very useful selection tool. With it you can select an area by tracing its edge. To select properly (e.g. the entire outline of a person), it is preferable to zoom in slightly and to work by regions. The graphic table often proves very useful and is indispensable for cropping. To select with the lasso, click a point on the edge of the region you want to select, then follow the edge with precision. To help you wield the lasso, use the zoom. See the section 'Retouching an image' for more information on cropping.

Rubber stamp tool

This is a grafting and retouching tool. Without it, it would be almost impossible to transplant one image onto another without noticing it! It would also be difficult to correct (or touch up) photographs that are damaged, aged, torn, etc. Only the rubber stamp can actually reproduce textures. It samples the colour and the texture and replicates them elsewhere. It features numerous options. It is known in **Paint Shop Pro** as the clone brush.

Moving tools

Zoom tool

To retouch an image properly, it is best to think (and see) big. Some software (including Photoshop) can enlarge up to 1600%. It thus becomes possible to correct tiny imperfections. To return to the initial image, just double-click on the *Magnifier* icon. When you click on the magnifier, you are in 'zoom' mode. Every time you click, you enlarge the image (up to the limit of 1600%). Note that you can 'zoom out' if you keep the [Alt] key down while clicking.

Note that the status bar displays the zoom value (here: 300%).

Hand tool

As long as the image occupies the entire window, you do not need a 'hand'. However, as soon as you enlarge the image, part of it may be out of the window and you will need to drag it regularly within the window. To access the hand tool, click its icon. As you will probably use this tool often, try to remember this shortcut: whatever tool you may be using, hold down the space bar; the hand appears and remains until you release the space bar.

In our example, the elephant, at 300%, is larger than the Photoshop window. Click on the hand, then drag across the window, so that the trunk disappears and part of the body can be seen instead.

Masking tools

Eraser tool

A very useful tool which does exactly what its name suggests. You can choose its thickness and its shape. When an image has several layers, the eraser is applied only to the selected layer.

Dodge tool

In Photoshop, the dodge tool is used to simulate an increase or a decrease of the photographic exposure during the printing process. This tool is also used to touch up shadows and highlights. Click on an area you want to brighten, for example. To accentuate the brightness, hold the the mouse button down.

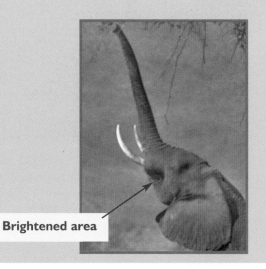

Brightened area

Smudge tool

The smudge tool acts like a finger on fresh paint... It is a masking tool used – as in painting – to mask areas that are too sharp. The smudge tool creates a 'soft-focus effect'. It is often used to give an impression of movement (or speed) to an image, such as a car, a plane or even an elephant!

Blur/sharpen tools

These two tools are available from the same Photoshop button (to go from one to the other, click on the button while pressing the [Alt] key). The blur tool desaturates the pixels, thus making part of an image less sharp. The sharpen tool, on the other hand, makes the pixels more intense and thus accentuates the sharpness of the object. Just select one of the tools and then go over the area you want to make sharper or softer, keeping the button of the mouse held down. The longer you keep the button pressed, the more powerful the effect.

Original

Blurred

Sharpened

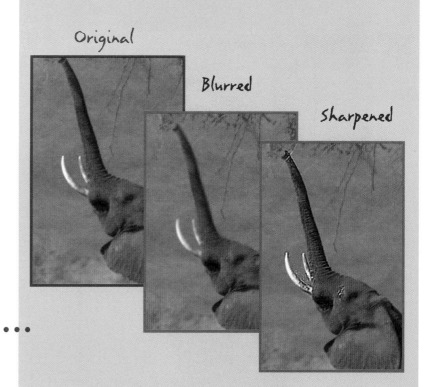

Pencil tool

This tool is used to draw lines of variable thickness. The outlines are sharp. The colour of the line must have been selected beforehand (e.g. by using the eyedropper). To draw a line with the pencil, select the tool, click the starting point of the line, hold the mouse button down and drag across. Release the button to end the line.

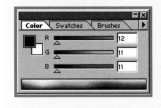

To select a colour, you can either use the eyedropper, use the swatches (just click on a colour to select it), or compose a colour with the basic settings (additive colour mixing, RGB scale). These last two windows open with the commands *Window/ Show Swatches* and *Show Color*.

Paintbrush tool

The paintbrush tool is used for the same purpose as the pencil: to draw lines. However, the paintbrush has special characteristics: the line it paints is smooth and merges into the background. You can use it with the 'Wet edges' option. In this case, the line is translucent and the edges darker, as if you were using watercolours. To draw a line close up with the paintbrush, select the tool, click the starting point of the line, hold the mouse button down, drag across, then release the button when you have reached the end of the line.

Airbrush tool

The airbrush simulates working with a spray gun. The lines it draws are less sharp than those of a brush or a pencil. They are semi-transparent. The airbrush reacts to the length of time the button of the mouse is pressed. As long as it is pressed, the spray gun keeps spraying ink (even if you don't move it). To draw a line with the airbrush, select the tool, click the starting point of the line, keep the the mouse button held down, and then draw the line by dragging across. Remain at a fixed location if you want part of the line to be denser.

Changing the line width

You may opt for a finer or thicker line, as well as a sharper or more blurred line, with the *Window/Show Brushes* command. Click on the thickness you want for the tool.

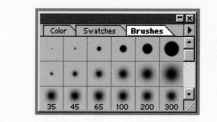

Eyedropper tool

A tool used to select colours: click on any pixel of an image, and the colour of the pixel is selected. It is even possible to obtain a colour from a mix of three or five adjacent pixels. The colour selected can then be used by one of the drawing tools, like the Paint bucket. The selected colour and the background colour are displayed in the toolbar.

Retouching an image

Until now, photographs printed on paper coated with photographic emulsion were exactly the shot you had taken, down to an individual grain. There was nothing you could do about the imperfections: finger prints, a huge lorry that passed by just as you snapped your son playing with the dog, over-exposure, a roll of film that had turned yellow, scratches on the negative (and their traces on the photograph), etc. Today, the situation is different if you can transfer your photographs to a computer. Retouching an image means restoring some of its lost quality; you can erase finger prints, mask scratches and carry out other repairs. Retouching an image also involves fiddling with contrast and brightness so that under-exposure and over-exposure are now a thing of the past. Retouching an image also means reviving colours that have faded or cropping a photograph in order to focus attention on the main subject.

The retouching tools also enable you to tinker with images. You can crop a section of the photograph, for example, to remove it and place it against a new background. Using the tools described earlier, you can alter the sharpness of the edges, so that the pasted selection fits perfectly into its new environment. And you can also have some fun tinkering with the shadows of the pasted selection so that they match those of the original photograph. You can do all of this within **Adobe Photoshop**.

Checklist

You will use this dialog box essentially with over- or under-exposed images.

1. Click the *Image/Adjust/Brightness/Contrast* command.

2. Use the cursor to increase the brightness (for an under-exposed image) or to reduce it (for an over-exposed image). You can also type a value in the corresponding text box.

3. Use the cursor to adjust the contrast. Under-exposed images (dark images) often have too little contrast: the colours cannot be distinguished clearly. It is better to increase the contrast. For over-exposed images, you will usually have to reduce the contrast.

4. Tick this box to preview the effect of the changes right away.

5. When you are happy with the result, click *OK* to confirm the settings.

Changing brightness and the contrast

Image/Adjust/Brightness/Contrast

① Click the Image/Adjust/Brightness/Contrast command.

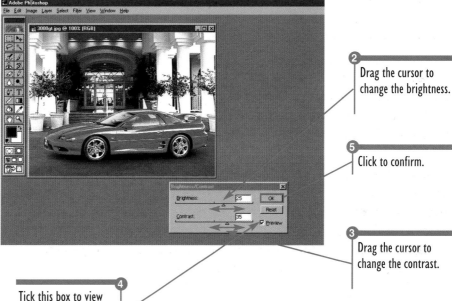

② Drag the cursor to change the brightness.

⑤ Click to confirm.

③ Drag the cursor to change the contrast.

④ Tick this box to view the changes.

Note that the cursors are reset to 0 as soon as you close this window. If you open it again, you will no longer see the reference values.

In Paint Shop Pro, click Colours/Adjust/Brightness/Contrast.

Tips for changing brightness and contrast ············

Original

Let's start with an image that is under-exposed, as is the case here. The original photograph is too dark, and the colours are consequently particularly faded. This is all the more unfortunate as normally the red should be vivid and the yellow 'bursting.'

A bit too much

Do not increase the brightness excessively, as the colours would fade for lack of contrast. If you then increased the contrast, you would get an image that has nothing natural left. Here, brightness and contrast were increased by 50%.

Corrected

Set the brightness and contrast to 25 and 35 respectively and the result is satisfactory.

Far too much

If you exaggerate this increase, you get a deliberately over-exposed image, in which the brightest colours stand out. Such a photograph could be used as the basis for a company logo used as letterhead watermark, for example.
In this case:
brightness: 75;
contrast: 65.

Checklist

1. Click the *Image/Adjust/ Color balance* command.

2. Click to select the tones to be adjusted (start with midtones, which are usually the most prevalent).

3. Move the appropriate sliding cursor to suit your needs (if, for example, the image is too yellow, move the third sliding cursor to 30, towards the blue). You can move all three cursors if necessary.

4. Tick the preview box to view the changes to the image instantly.

5. Click to confirm your choices.

••••• **Note** •••••

Depending on the outcome of the changes in the balance of midtones, you can also adjust the highlights and the shadows.

Correcting the colours of an image

Image/Adjust/Color balance

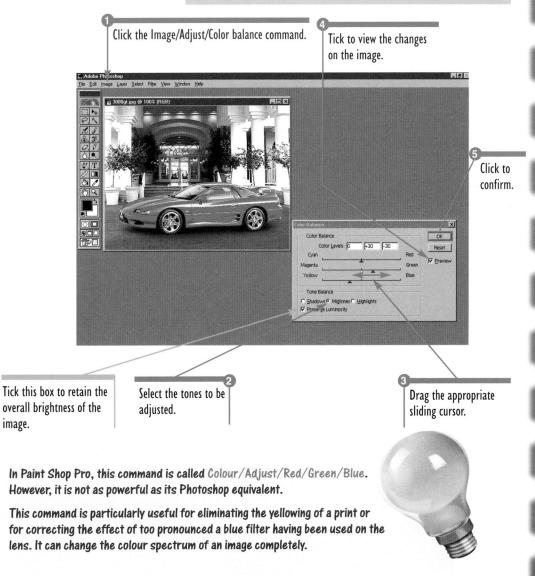

1 Click the Image/Adjust/Color balance command.

4 Tick to view the changes on the image.

5 Click to confirm.

Tick this box to retain the overall brightness of the image.

2 Select the tones to be adjusted.

3 Drag the appropriate sliding cursor.

In Paint Shop Pro, this command is called Colour/Adjust/Red/Green/Blue. However, it is not as powerful as its Photoshop equivalent.

This command is particularly useful for eliminating the yellowing of a print or for correcting the effect of too pronounced a blue filter having been used on the lens. It can change the colour spectrum of an image completely.

Cropping an image

Marquee and Image/Crop

① Select the marquee tool.

③ Click the command to crop.

② Draw a selection frame.

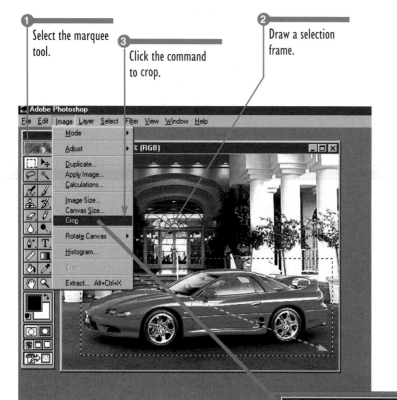

④ Only the content of the selection remains.

① Select the marquee tool.

② Draw a selection frame around the area you wish to keep.

③ Click *Image/Crop*.

④ The content of the frame is kept. The rest of the image is deleted.

Checklist

Cropping a subject means selecting it, in order to move it elsewhere or to modify it. The lasso tool is found in most retouching programs.

1. Click the Lasso tool. The mouse pointer turns into a lasso.

2. Zoom in on the image until the subject fills the entire window.

3. Click anywhere on the subject outline and, keeping the button of the mouse held down, follow precisely the outline of the subject.

4. When you get back to the starting point, release the button of the mouse. You have now selected the subject.

5. You can copy the subject in order to paste it on another layer, for example, or reverse the selection and erase the new one in order to keep only the subject.

Lasso

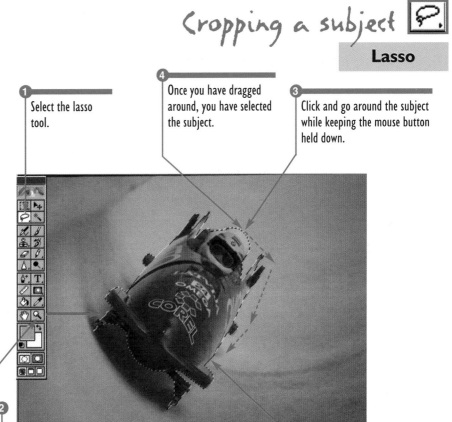

1. Select the lasso tool.

4. Once you have dragged around, you have selected the subject.

3. Click and go around the subject while keeping the mouse button held down.

2. Zoom in on the subject to be cropped.

5. Copy the selection, or erase it, as required.

Photoshop also provides a special 'polygonal' lasso. To use it, click the lasso tool and keep the mouse button held down. A small toolbar is displayed. Click the polygonal lasso button. With this tool, you must click at each change of direction. It then automatically draws a straight line between the points on which you clicked. You don't need to follow the exact outline while keeping the button held down. Click several times to get a fine curve (which is, in fact, made of many small straight lines). When you get back to your starting point, you have selected the object. In Paint Shop Pro, change the Lasso type to 'Point to point' in the control panel.

Cropping a subject against a background

Magic Wand, then Select/Inverse

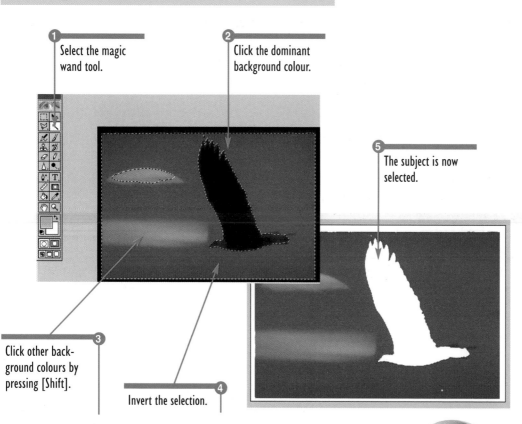

① Select the magic wand tool.

② Click the dominant background colour.

⑤ The subject is now selected.

③ Click other background colours by pressing [Shift].

④ Invert the selection.

This tool is faster than the lasso, but must be used on a plain background. To achieve a good result with this cropping tool, the subject must be of a different colour to the background. To get good results, the subject must not contain any colour identical to that of the background (because the magic wand selects all dots of one particular colour). Some background colours (like the orange, in our example) may not be selected with the rest of the background (here, the red). They are simply too different. You can add them to the selection by clicking them while holding the [Shift] key pressed. You just add to the selection.

Checklist

This procedure makes it possible to select a subject that appears on a plain background, or one that is made of three or four colours at the most.

① Click to select the magic wand.

② Click the main background colour. In the illustration, red was selected.

③ If areas are not selected, click them while holding the [Shift] key down. The areas are added to the selection.

④ The entire background being selected, you can invert the selection (using the *Select/Inverse* command). The background is no longer selected, while the subject is.

⑤ Now that the subject is selected, you can copy it, on the same image or onto another one.

Applying special effects

Adobe Photoshop, like most other image editing software, is delivered with an impressive set of filters and special effects. You can use them to enhance images, impressing people with your production. Or you can use them simply to have fun. With special effects, you can add a shadow to an object, surround another with a bright halo, etc.

There are corrective filters and destructive filters. The former simulate the action of filters used in photography to correct the lighting, the perspective or the sharpness of a picture, or to improve the overall quality of the image. Destructive filters change the architecture of the image to achieve the desired effect. If you want to keep a copy of the original image, do not forget to save it under another name before applying the filter. The application of a filter may take from a few seconds to several hours, depending on the size of the image, the complexity of the filter and the speed of your PC.

REMARK

The filters supplied with Paint Shop Pro are mainly corrective, rather than destructive. They are available from the lower part of the Image menu. There are fewer special effects in this program than in Photoshop.

Applying an outer glow

Layer/Effects/Outer glow

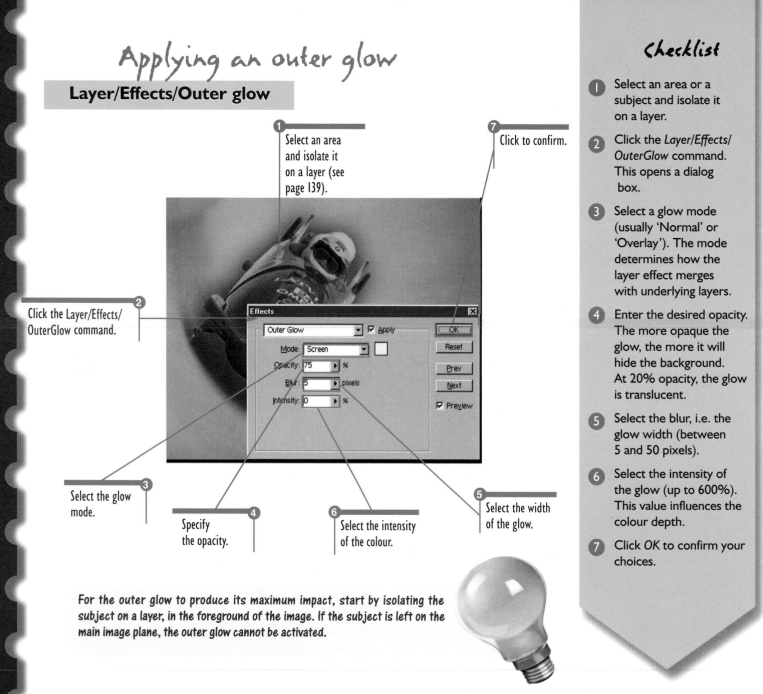

① Select an area and isolate it on a layer (see page 139).

⑦ Click to confirm.

② Click the Layer/Effects/OuterGlow command.

Effects

Outer Glow ▾   ☑ Apply   OK

Mode: Screen ▾   Reset

Opacity: 75 ▸ %   Prev

Blur: 5 ▸ pixels   Next

Intensity: 0 ▸ %   ☑ Preview

③ Select the glow mode.

④ Specify the opacity.

⑥ Select the intensity of the colour.

⑤ Select the width of the glow.

For the outer glow to produce its maximum impact, start by isolating the subject on a layer, in the foreground of the image. If the subject is left on the main image plane, the outer glow cannot be activated.

Checklist

① Select an area or a subject and isolate it on a layer.

② Click the *Layer/Effects/ OuterGlow* command. This opens a dialog box.

③ Select a glow mode (usually 'Normal' or 'Overlay'). The mode determines how the layer effect merges with underlying layers.

④ Enter the desired opacity. The more opaque the glow, the more it will hide the background. At 20% opacity, the glow is translucent.

⑤ Select the blur, i.e. the glow width (between 5 and 50 pixels).

⑥ Select the intensity of the glow (up to 600%). This value influences the colour depth.

⑦ Click *OK* to confirm your choices.

Checklist

1. Select a field or a subject and isolate it on a layer.

2. Click the *Layer/Effects/ Drop shadow* command. This opens a dialog box.

3. Select a shadow mode. 'Product' mode gives the best results.

4. Select the opacity (see preceding page).

5. Select the angle of the shadow in relation to the subject.

6. Select the distance separating the shadow from the subject (in pixels).

7. Select a blur (the shadow diffusion effect).

8. Select the intensity (the 'depth') of the shadow.

9. Click *OK* to confirm the shadow settings.

Applying a drop shadow on a subject

Layer/Effects/Drop shadow

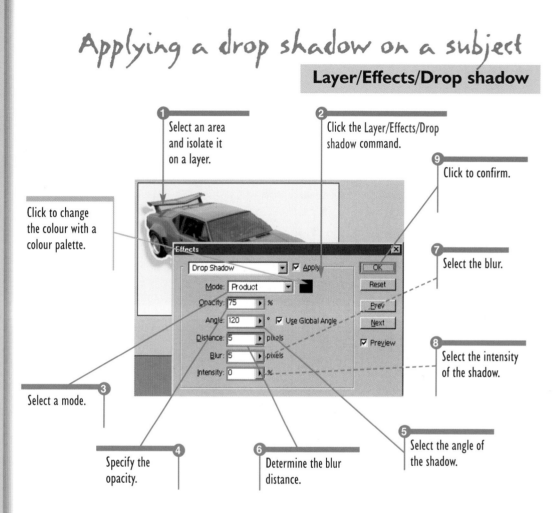

Select an area and isolate it on a layer.

Click the Layer/Effects/Drop shadow command.

Click to confirm.

Click to change the colour with a colour palette.

Select the blur.

Select the intensity of the shadow.

Select a mode.

Specify the opacity.

Determine the blur distance.

Select the angle of the shadow.

It is possible to copy and paste a special effect you have applied previously. Photoshop uses an internal clipboard that has no influence on the Windows clipboard. To copy and paste an effect, select the layer in which the effect has been applied previously. Use the Layer/Effects/Copy Effects command. Go to another layer (in the same file or in another), then use Layer/Effects/Paste Effects. This procedure cannot be carried out if the image has been flattened (if the layers have been merged). It is therefore essential to save images in Photoshop format in order to keep independent layers.

143

Changing the colour of an effect

This indicator displays the new colour at the top, and the previously selected colour at the bottom.

① Click to select a colour.

② Click OK to confirm.

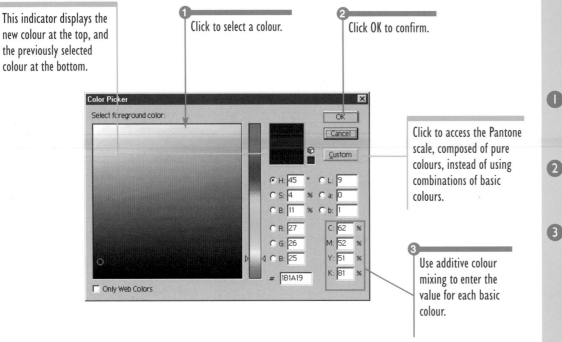

Click to access the Pantone scale, composed of pure colours, instead of using combinations of basic colours.

③ Use additive colour mixing to enter the value for each basic colour.

Checklist

You access the colour picker from the tool palette or from any colour selection window in the dialogue boxes (for example, the effects window, described in the preceding pages).

To select a new colour

① Click in the spectrum. The selected colour appears in the transparent circle.

② Click OK to confirm.

To select a colour with precision

③ Use the value of each component of the colour. You can use RGB, CMYK, Lab or HLS scales. You should use this procedure if you are working according to precise specifications.

Examples of effects

Drop shadow
Product mode, orange colour, opacity: 75%, angle: 120°, distance: 35 pixels, blur: 25 pixels, intensity: 40%

Inner shadow
Product mode, black colour, opacity: 75%, angle: 120°, distance: 25 pixels, blur: 25 pixels, intensity: 50%

Inner glow
Overlay mode, green colour, opacity: 50%, blur 25 pixels, intensity: 100%, option 'Edge'

Outer glow
Normal mode, blue colour, opacity: 75%, blur: 25 pixels, intensity: 40%

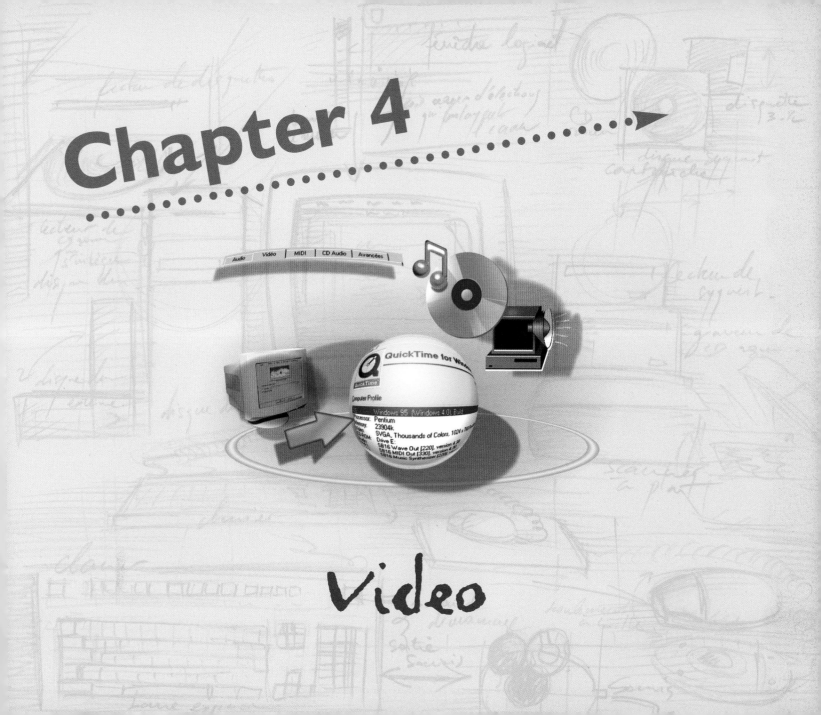

Chapter 4

Video

Introduction to video editing

A multimedia computer can be used as a video-editing console. Images recorded with a video camera can be captured by computer and displayed on screen. With the help of a specialised program (such as **Adobe Premiere** or **Final Cut Pro**), you can edit a video sequence, deleting images, adding filters and transition effects between shots, and also applying special effects etc. When the computer-assisted video editing is completed, you can add sound, then record the movie on the medium of your choice: a computer storage device, a **VHS** tape, etc.

Recording the image

An image recorded with an analogue camera is transformed into a series of horizontal lines. In the **PAL** format, each image is divided into 625 lines. In this process, which is called scanning, each dot of the line is given a brightness value. A black and white image is obtained by recording only the brightness. To obtain colour, another scan must be carried out to separate the three basic colours. To record motion smoothly, a camera must be able to record at least 18 images per second. Today, 25 or 30 images are recorded per second, but this was not always the case. The first capture cards, for instance, recorded only 15 images per second, giving the film a jerky motion.

HOW TO

Video editing on a computer requires:
- ✔ A powerful multimedia computer equipped with a maximum of RAM (128 Mb recommended).
- ✔ A video camera.
- ✔ A video capture card (specialised expansion card).
- ✔ Editing software.
- ✔ A large-capacity medium to store the edited film.

Video connection

The digital video camera is at the centre of a new communication technology (instant film) and can be hooked up directly (or indirectly) to many video or IT devices. The **PC** or the **Macintosh** are, for a video maker, just a device attached to his/her camera, as are the video printer and title editing console.

Connecting camcorders and videotape recorders may appear quite complex. In fact, it's simply a matter of remembering that there is specific wiring for audio, video, editing and digital. Also, standard devices tend to be equipped with cheap cables, with more expensive ones used for professional equipment. Furthermore, different names are at times used for the same plugs. Finally, analogue video editing is made more difficult by a real lack of compatibility between cabling systems of different brands, which is itself a good reason for opting for digital editing, which uses only one type of cable! The table below should clarify matters. Ideally, memorise it.

HOW TO

Various devices can be connected to a good videotape console. Altough it has BNC, RAC, Ushiden, Lanc, JLIP and other such connectors, the videotape console shown below does not have a FireWire input for digital signals. Digital video-tape recorders are still rather new and expensive. This is especially troublesome because most digital camcorders will not record from an external signal (the IN input is blocked for customs and tax reasons).

To make things easy for everyone, there is a colour code that indicates the type of connector immediately:

Yellow: for video.
Red: for audio.
White: for audio.
Blue: for editing (Lanc (Propietary socket for interfacing with other gear).
Black: for audio or video.

Video connection standards

'All' digital connection

FireWire

This is the only standard! A tiny connector, a thin cable.

Analogue audio connection

Video audio jack
SCART (Euro-AV).

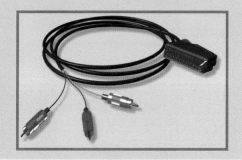

Analogue video connection

BNC
S-Video or Ushiden or Y/C
Video audio jack
S-VHS

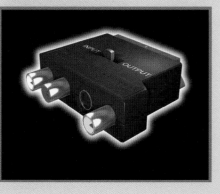

Analogue editing connection

Unfortunately, there is no standard, here. Every manufacturer has his own type of plug when he does not choose an infrared connection or a specialised editing table. For analogue editing, therefore, it is preferable to choose devices (videotape recorder, editing table, etc.) which are all of the same brand.

Incompatibility problems disappear with digital editing, as the PC replaces all other devices and connections are carried out through standard plugs (analogue S-Video, digital FireWire, etc.).

Video camera

A digital camera is not essential for digital editing. All you need is a conventional camcorder and a video capture card. However, digital quality is superior to analogue and all recent digital cameras have the connections required for moving to 'all digital', from shooting, to playing of digital cassettes. So, if you can afford digital, do not hesitate.

Digital Video or DV camcorders record the image directly in digital format by converting the analogue signal from the CCD sensors (the 'retina of the camcorder') into a digital signal. They have all the connections required to let you view images on a standard television set or on a computer, provided you have a specific capture or transfer card. When video editing on the computer is completed, all you have to do is transfer the file to the digital videotape recorder or back to the digital camera. The transfer to an analogue cassette can be carried out from the camcorder (which features full analogue connection) or from certain digital cards that also feature this connection (see the chapter devoted to capture cards). Unfortunately, most digital camcorders sold in the UK do not have an **IN** input, which means that they cannot be used as videotape recorders. As **IN** access was simply deprogrammed on some videotape recorders (the Sony, for example), it is possible to reprogram it, but this is a complex and risky procedure. If done incorrectly, the video camera can be permanently damaged.

REMARK

A camcorder is a device that captures and records the movement of light. To do this, it has four basic components:

An optical system.

Control mechanisms.

One (or more) CCD sensor(s).

A motor drive (to forward the tape, move the optical system, etc.).

Video standards

Standards

PAL (Phase Alternation by Line) format

This is the European form of colour image coding, which reduces the risk of errors at hue level. The resolution of a PAL image is 768 x 576 pixels, which is superior to the standard of 14' VGA computer screens (this explains why, for video, the graphic display card and the screen must be of a quality superior to VGA). A 17' screen is ideal.

The SECAM format (which stands for 'Sequential Colour and Memory' system)

This is the television standard used in France, in the countries of the former USSR and in some African countries (sometimes with modifications). The SECAM standard is not recognised in video (so there are no SECAM camcorders) because it is very difficult to edit a video signal using this coding.

Digital video standard

This is known as DV for short. DV camcorders store the image directly in digital format using **CCD** sensors. The specific digital connection is called FireWire (or **IEEE 1394**). It is a very small connection that uses a very thin cable, and it is the fastest connection at the moment. The main characteristics of a DV camera are a horizontal resolution of 500 points per line (compared with 250 points per line for VHS and 400 points per line for the S-VHS and Hi-8 formats); no colour bleeding; sound recording of audio compact disc quality; the possibility of filming in 16/9, the new widescreen television format; and, above all, no degradation during editing and copying.

Capturing a video image

A special expansion card is needed to capture video signals. This card is linked to the video camera, from which it receives the signals, and to the internal components of the computer. In order to capture analogue signals (as with most video cameras at present), you need an analogue card. If the signals are digital, then you need a digital video capture card.

'Analogue/digital' video capture cards turn the signal of an analogue camcorder into a digital signal, the only one that can be understood and used by the computer. In other words, these cards can receive the signal from a VHS, S-VH, 8 mm or Hi-8 camcorder and convert it into a digital signal that can be used by video editing software. Once the film has been edited, the digital signal can then be converted back into an analogue signal and sent to a videotape recorder, or simply saved on a **CD-ROM**. Analogue/digital conversion requires a very fast hard disk because the signal that leaves the camcorder is not yet compressed and the data flow is consequently considerable.

'All digital' video capture cards, as their name indicates, process only digital signals. These cards can only receive a signal from a **DV** camera (**FireWire**). The output signal will likewise be digital. Therefore, they can only work with a digital videotape recorder or with a **DV** camcorder with the adapted input port. If an analogue output signal is also to be produced (e.g. S-Video), a digital card must be used in conjunction with an analogue/digital card.

TIP

You can do without an expansion card by using an interface between the PC (USB port) and the camera. This package plays the role of a dispatcher (with many cables coming in and as many going out). It is driven by software installed in the PC. Some interfaces come with a card that must be inserted in the PC. We then talk of a connection kit (for example, Iomega Buz).

Editing software

Until recently, the only way to edit a video (i.e. build a film from rushes shot at different times) was to use an editing table or a videotape recorder (in fact, it was preferable to have two videotape recorders, and the connectors were compatible only if the two machines were of the same brand). You also had to have an editing table, a titler, a mixer, a module for special effects, etc. It was long, complicated and expensive. Then computers were used as simple editing tables, to store the beginning and end of sequences and to drive the videotape recorders and the camcorders. Now, computers are powerful enough to do without the videotape recorder and all its peripherals. Not only did the computer replace all the peripherals but, on top of that, the image quality is no longer affected by the editing (as of course, the original is never used).

The most common editing software used by amateur video-makers is currently Adobe Premiere (current version: 5.1). Most camcorders or capture cards are delivered with a copy of this software. In addition to editing, Premiere also features filters and numerous special effects that can be applied to the sequence. These effects are generally used for the transition between shots or takes.

HOW TO

Application of a transition effect between two sequences, using Adobe Premiere.

TIP
Premiere is not the only editing software. QuickTime is particularly worth mentioning. This is a 'small multimedia' operating system, which can also be used to carry out small editing tasks easily. It is described in chapter 5, which is devoted to important multimedia utilities.

Video storage media

Once video editing is completed, you can record the final document on a **DV** cassette, by linking the computer and the digital videotape recorder or digital camcorder via the FireWire interface. Digital videotape recorders are still very expensive, but, to be used as a recorder, a camcorder must have an **IN DV** input, which is not the case with most consumer **DV** camcorders.

The movie can also be transfered to a cassette on an analogue videotape recorder (**VHS, VHS-C, Hi-8**) through an appropriate connection, converting the signals into analogue video format (composite, S-Video or YUV).

The movie can also be saved on a computer storage device (Bernouilli Jazz, CD-ROM, etc.) by converting the file into a proper video format (Quicktime, Video for Windows, etc.). The movie is then saved in the same way as any other computer generated document. If the recording is to be played on another system, certain settings may need to be adjusted during the recording.

TIP

Another storage medium is bound to become the standard in the near future: the mini DV cassette.

The size of a matchbox (66 x 48 x 12 mm), this cassette is much smaller than the VHS-C or Hi-8 cassette that is used in analogue camcorders. The tape also moves much more rapidly (36 km/h). It is available in two formats: 30 and 60 minutes. Some models are fitted with an auxiliary memory chip used to store data for subsequent editing, such as reference marks, time codes, etc. This chip (which is 4 to 16 Kb Flash RAM) uses four metal contacts on the side of the cassette. All digital cameras can play these cassettes but not all have access to the contents of the chip.

HOW TO

To view images edited at home, the medium of reference will remain, for some time yet, the VHS video cassette.

Checklist

1. Use the command to open the Windows media player. The registered video formats are: Video for Windows (AVI) and ActiveMovie (MOV, M1v, AU, etc.).

2. Click *File/Open* to locate the video excerpt to play.

3. Select the type of file you want to open: in general, Video for Windows.

4. Click to open the selected file.

5. The movie is displayed in thumbnail format, in a separate window below the window of the player. You can now play it.

Start/Programs/Accessories/Entertainment/Media Player

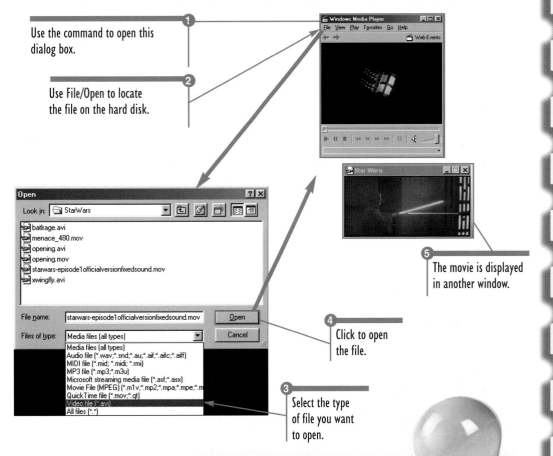

Use the command to open this dialog box.

Use File/Open to locate the file on the hard disk.

The movie is displayed in another window.

Click to open the file.

Select the type of file you want to open.

If you double-click the icon of a video file, Windows opens a window identical to that presented on this page, but accompanied by two main control buttons (Start and Stop). The multimedia player will not be opened.

▥ Playing a video file

Start/Programs/Accessories/Entertainment/Media Player

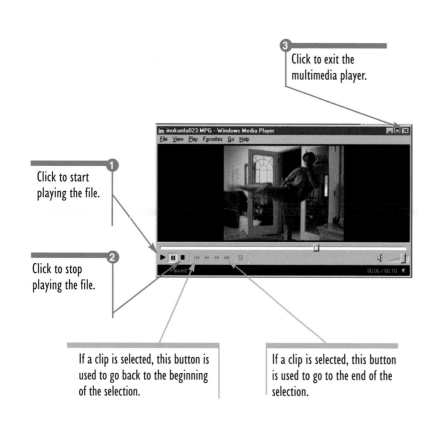

❸ Click to exit the
multimedia player.

❶ Click to start
playing the file.

❷ Click to stop
playing the file.

If a clip is selected, this button is
used to go back to the beginning
of the selection.

If a clip is selected, this button
is used to go to the end of the
selection.

Checklist

The multimedia player
control buttons
correspond to those
of any CD player.
(For more details,
see page 83).

❶ Click to start playing
the file.

❷ Click to stop playing
the file.

❸ Click to exit the
multimedia player.

••••• *Hint* •••••

To play an extract
endlessly, tick the
option *Repeat forever*
in the *View/Options*
dialog box. This option
can be useful to create
a touch screen kiosk.

Checklist

You can change the video display options. Windows offers only two alternatives: a thumbnail format and full screen. However, a video image has a specific resolution. It can only display a limited number of pixels. In thumbnail format the display is sharp, clear and flawless, although you have to concentrate to view the clip. In full screen, the same image is enormously enlarged and its quality is impaired. Each pixel is shown as a square with a 5 mm side.

1. Select a display format.
2. Click *Apply* to view the difference.
3. Click *OK* to confirm.

Changing video display settings

Multimedia Player/Devices/Properties

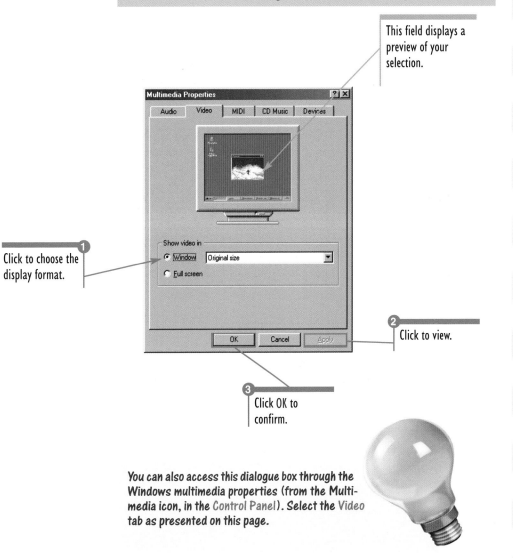

This field displays a preview of your selection.

Click to choose the display format. ①

② Click to view.

③ Click OK to confirm.

You can also access this dialogue box through the Windows multimedia properties (from the Multimedia icon, in the Control Panel). Select the Video tab as presented on this page.

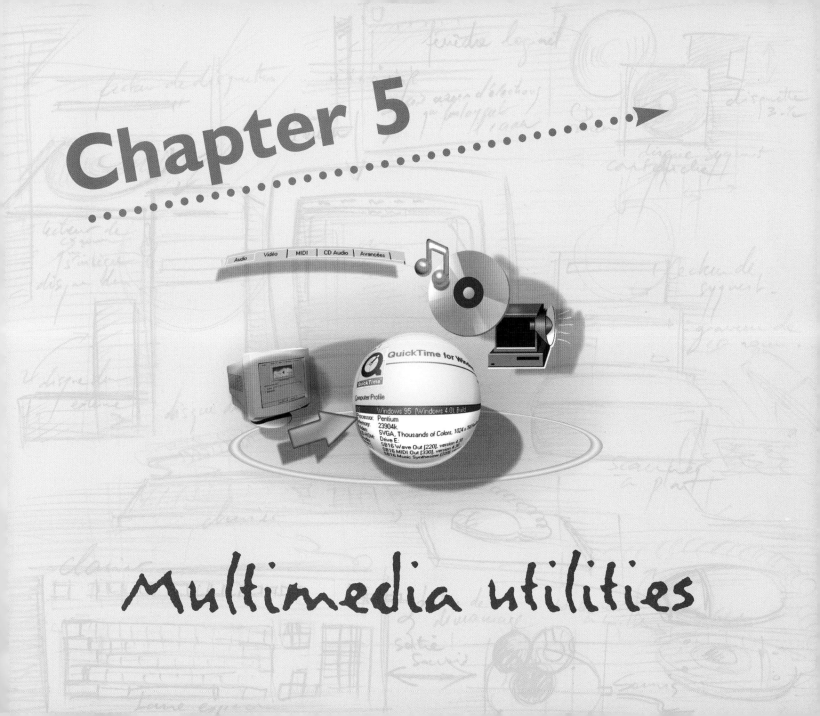

Chapter 5

Multimedia utilities

CD writers...

It is difficult to discuss multimedia without mentioning **CD** recorders. They have proliferated as their cost has dropped to within everyone's reach. It is now not only possible but also inexpensive to duplicate software, games, sound and, of course, audio CDs. You don't need to be a computer specialist to copy CDs, as **CD** writers usually come with software that is easy to use. This usually includes a **CD** copier (to copy the entire **CD** inserted in the **CD-ROM** drive), a data copier (to copy data from other sources such as a hard disk), an audio **CD** copier (to copy an audio **CD** from the **CD-ROM** drive) and a **CD** eraser (to erase the contents of a **CD-RW**).

Other software may also be included, which facilitates the creation of **CD** case inserts or **CD** labels. The programs presented in the following pages are from Adaptec, and are supplied with the **HP CD** recorders. They are very similar to other software currently available on the market.

TIP

In order to use a CD-ROM writer, you need blank CDs. There are different types of recordable CDs. A CD-R (where the 'R' stands for 'recordable') can be written to only once. Data is then stored on astable medium that cannot be erased. A CD-RW (where 'RW' stands for 'rewritable') can be written to several times, provided it is erased before new data is recorded. It is also possible to write several sessions on a single CD. It all depends on the recorder purchased: some accept CD-R only, others write on CD-RW as well.

Copying a CD

Start/CD Creator/CD Copier (for example)

Click here to access the advanced properties of the CD Copier (see next page).

1 Select the CD-ROM reader to copy from.

3 Select a copying procedure.

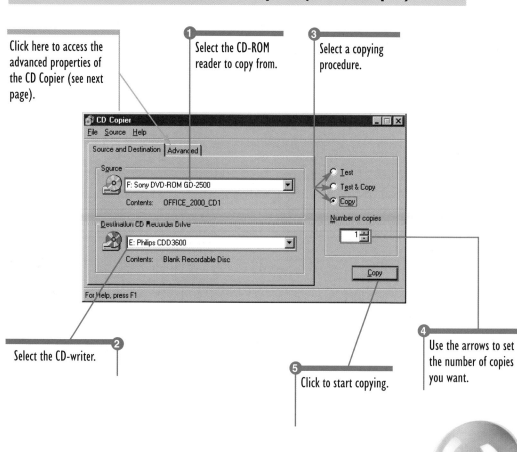

Select the CD-writer. **2**

5 Click to start copying.

4 Use the arrows to set the number of copies you want.

To copy a CD successfully, you need a CD-ROM reader with a minimum speed of 30x. If the speed is lower than 30x, the data flow may be too slow for the recorder. The process will then abort.

Checklist

1 Select the source of the data, i.e. the drive in which the CD is inserted.

2 Select the destination for the data, i.e. the CD-recorder in which the blank CD is inserted.

3 Choose to run a test only, a test followed by the real copy, or the copy only with no test phase. In most cases, you will select the *Copy* option.

4 Set the number of copies to be made (usually 1).

5 Click *Copy* to start copying.

•••••• **Note** •••••

With this program, you copy the entire contents of the original CD, in a single session. If you wish to copy tracks from several CDs onto a single CD, use the special utility program that can copy selected data.

Advanced settings

Advanced tab

Select the lowest speed available, unless you have to meet impossible deadlines. A low recording speed usually produces a more stable CD than a high speed. The work is more precise and subsequent problems are less likely.

Checklist

1. Select the Recorder speed.

2. If you have not already done so, choose to run a test only, a test followed by a real copy, or the copy only with no test phase.

3. Click to launch the copying process.

Checklist

1. Click to disconnect the recorder. The driver's icon disappears from the Windows taskbar.

2. Click OK to confirm the disconnection, unless the window closes automatically.

3. To reconnect the recorder afterwards, click Connect.

Connecting or disconnecting the drive

Start/Programs/CD creator/CD connector

This option is useful for saving system resources. The recorder is connected automatically at startup. The driver icon appears on the taskbar, which means that it is loaded in RAM, therefore occupying part of the memory. If you disconnect the drive, you can free several hundred kb of RAM for other applications.

Copying data from several sources: a flow chart

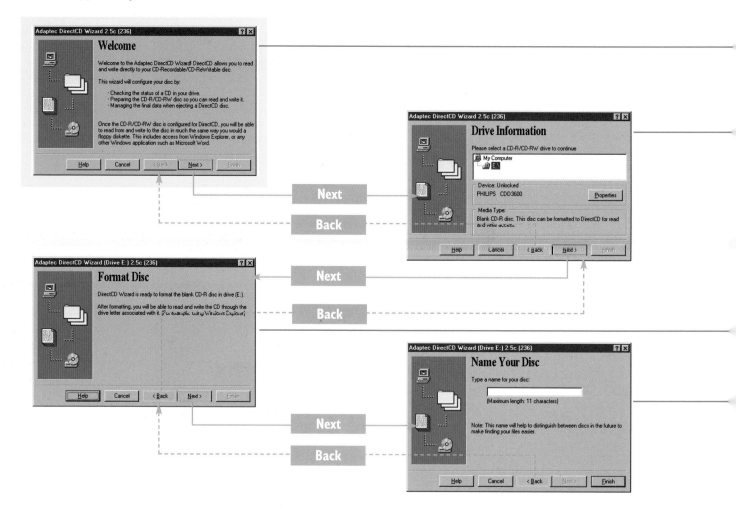

Theory

Adaptec DirectCD
Wizard first dialogue box.

Select the CD writer.
The program indicates
the status of the CD it
contains.

This page enables you to
format a blank CD for
use on your computer.

Give a name to the new
CD. Click *Finish*. You
must then indicate to the
program the location
of the data folder.

To copy an entire **CD-ROM** on a **CD-R**, use the **CD-copier**. The data will be copied directly from the **CD-ROM** reader to the **CD-recorder**, without being saved on the hard disk. If, on the other hand, you wish to write on a **CD** data coming from several sources, you need to store the data on a hard disk first.

This is because the program used to write to the **CD** is limited to a single session: it cannot stop to let you change **CDs**. If it could, it would mean that you would need to be present during the recording which takes a long time.

Copying data to the disk imposes several constraints. For one, you must have enough free disk space for the data you wish to copy. As the maximum capacity of a **CD** is **640 Mb**, it is best to have **700 Mb** free at all times. You must also defragment your hard disk regularly.* If the disk is fragmented, the program used to write on the **CD** needs to search for small pieces of data just about everywhere, increasing the possibility of errors.

Finally, deactivate any screen savers that may currently be running. A screen saver can interfere with the writing of data, making the **CD-R** unreadable. In the same way, deactivate all resident programs (the icons in the Windows taskbar): any anti-virus software (in particular), the Office shortcut bar, any connection to the Internet, etc.

* This procedure is described in the book on Windows 98, published in this series (in the section on System tools).

Recording an Audio CD: a flow chart

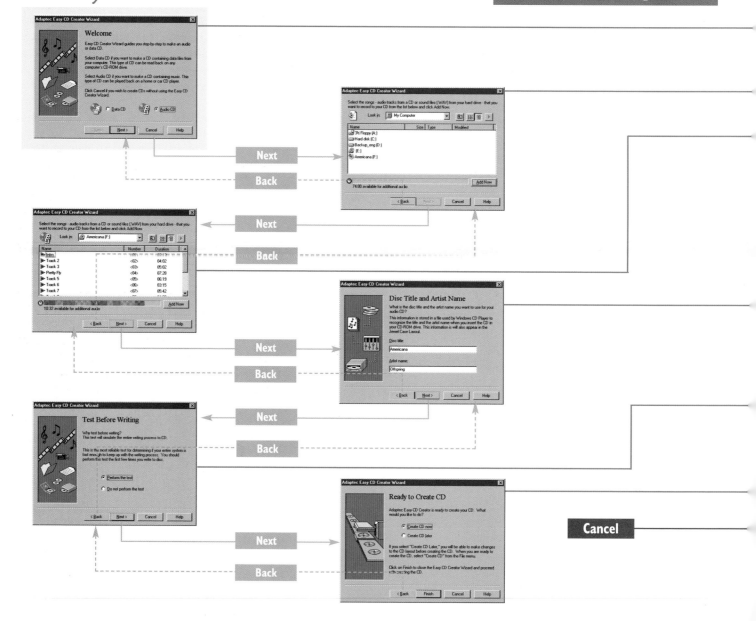

- The Adaptec Easy CD Creator Wizard first dialogue box.

- Select the audio CD you want to copy.

- Select the tracks you want to copy. The time remaining on the CD-R is indicated. You can copy the same track several times or select others. The order of the tracks is displayed in the Easy CD Creator Wizard window.

- Enter the name of the CD and of the artist.

- Click to test the CD copying before the real recording process. Recommended, but not compulsory.

- Click to start the recording process.

- Cancels the entire procedure.

The Easy CD Creator window lists all the selected tracks. To record them on the hard disk (see Theory), right-click a track, then click the command [*Prerecord* in *.wav* *file*]. The file must be named through a standard File save window.

Theory...

If it is possible to copy an entire **CD** at once, it is also possible to copy selected tracks from a single **CD**, or selected tracks from several **CDs**.

In the first case, use the audio **CD** recording wizard, which will ask you to select the tracks of the audio **CD** to be copied. Then follow the instructions of the wizard as illustrated on the opposite page. The principle is simple: identify the source of the music (the audio **CD**), select the tracks, enter a name for the **CD**, then start the recording process. The wizard is launched automatically, but you can always return to the general window by clicking *Cancel*.

In the second case, you must first copy each track from the **CDs** onto the hard disk. The tracks are recorded as *.wav* files (with **CD** quality, each second takes up about 200 kb on the hard disk). Tell the Easy CD Creator where to find the files to be written onto the blank **CD**. The recording is then carried out without using the **CD-ROM** drive: the program transfers the data from the hard disk to the **CD-R**. The defragmentation of the hard disk is, of course, very important for this procedure.

CHAPTER 5 : MULTIMEDIA UTILITIES

Erasing data from a CD

Start/Programs/Recorder/CD Eraser

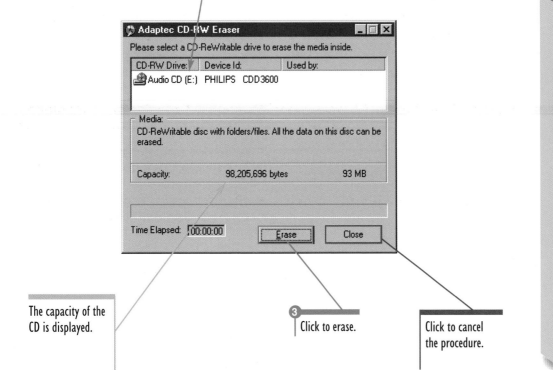

2 Select the CD-ROM writer that contains the CD-RW to erase.

Adaptec CD-RW Eraser

Please select a CD-ReWritable drive to erase the media inside.

CD-RW Drive:	Device Id:	Used by:
Audio CD (E:)	PHILIPS	CDD3600

Media:
CD-ReWritable disc with folders/files. All the data on this disc can be erased.

Capacity: 98,205,696 bytes 93 MB

Time Elapsed: 00:00:00   Erase   Close

The capacity of the CD is displayed.

3 Click to erase.

Click to cancel the procedure.

Checklist

1 Make sure you want to erase the entire contents of the CD. Use Windows Explorer, if necessary.

2 Select the CD-ROM writer.

3 Click *Erase* to start the erasing process. The program displays a progress bar window.

••••• **Note** •••••

Only CD-RWs (see tip box on the introductory page of this section) can be erased. The entire CD is erased… i.e. all data is lost.

Compressing data with WinZip
Start/Programs/WinZip

As we have already seen, compressing data reduces the size of the files without changing their contents or characteristics. To restore a compressed file to its initial state, you must decompress it with the program used to compress it, or a compatible program. The compressed files have a special file name extension, which corresponds to the compression program used. In the case of WinZip, the file name extension is .ZIP. WinZip rapidly emerged as the compression standard on the PC, to such an extent that compressed files are now referred to as 'zipped' files. Many files transferred across the Internet are zipped so that they can be downloaded faster. Files attached to e-mail messages are frequently zipped too, as are files saved on diskettes (where space is really limited). It is therefore essential to have access to WinZip (which is often pre-installed on new computers). Read the 'Tip' on this page.

There are several versions of WinZip such as WinZip 3.1 (version for Windows 3.1 running in 16-bit mode), and WinZip 6.2 (32-bit version for Windows 95, 98 and Windows NT). Both of them include PKZip and PKUnzip, the forefathers of WinZip, which were used to compress and decompress large **MS-DOS** files. The latest version, WinZip 7.0, is strongly recommended if you use Windows 95 or 98.

TIP

WinZip is a shareware program (you can use it free of charge for 21 days, but you then have to acquire a licence). You will find it on practically all CD-ROMs in computer magazines. Otherwise, you can download it from the WinZip web site:

http://www.winzip.com

If it was pre-installed on your new computer, you will not have to pay any licence fee.

WinZip offers two user interfaces: WinZip Classic, and WinZip Wizard. WinZip Classic displays the conventional interface of Windows applications with a toolbar, menus, etc.

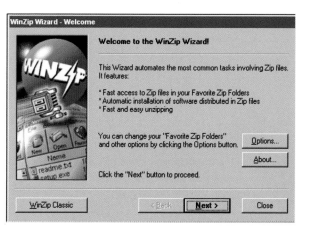

Compressing files with Winzip classic

File/New archive

1 Click File/New archive. A zipped file is also refered to as an 'archive'.

The size of the archive is 115 kb, whereas the size of the original files was 527 kb. The compression rate is displayed (as a percentage) in the WinZip window. 80% compression, for example, means, that a file that took up 100 kb before being zipped now takes up only 20 kb.

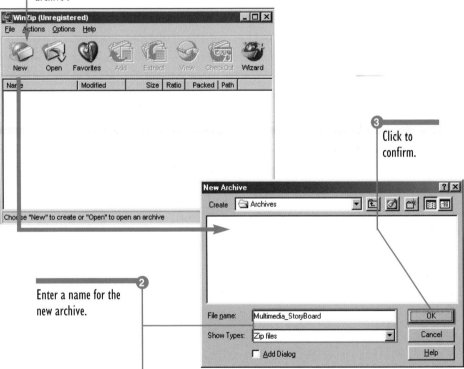

3 Click to confirm.

Enter a name for the new archive.

2

An archive is a single file. If several files have been zipped together, they become a single zipped file until they are uncompressed. To zip each file in a separate archive, you must create a new archive for each. This is a little tedious, but it is the only way.

Checklist

1 Click *File/New Archive* to create a new archive in which to store the compressed files. WinZip opens a dialogue box.

2 Enter the name for the file (always pick a name that is clear for you and for whoever will use the archive). Files you drag into this archive will automatically be compressed.

3 Click *OK* to confirm the creation of the new archive. WinZip then displays another dialogue box, through which you can locate the files you want to compress.

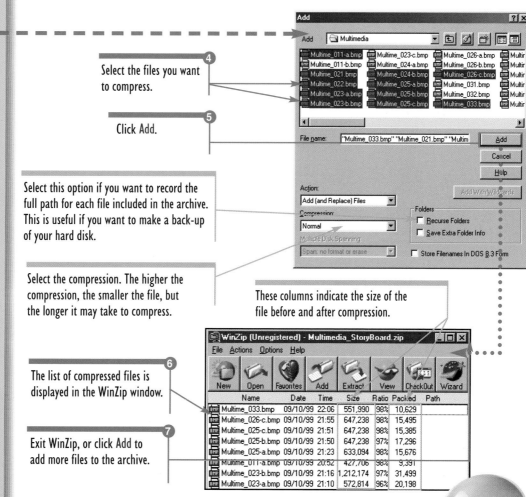

④ Select the files you wish to compress. To select several adjacent files, click the first one, then click the last one while holding down the [Shift] key. To select several non-adjacent files click the first, then click the others while holding the [Ctrl] key down.

⑤ When all files are selected, click *Add*. WinZip now displays its main window once again.

⑥ The list of compressed files in the archive is displayed. From the Windows Explorer point of view, there is only one file now: the archive, with its .ZIP extension.

⑦ If you wish, you may now exit WinZip. To add another file to the archive, click the *Add* icon. The 'Add' window is then open once again.

④ Select the files you want to compress.

⑤ Click Add.

Select this option if you want to record the full path for each file included in the archive. This is useful if you want to make a back-up of your hard disk.

Select the compression. The higher the compression, the smaller the file, but the longer it may take to compress.

These columns indicate the size of the file before and after compression.

⑥ The list of compressed files is displayed in the WinZip window.

⑦ Exit WinZip, or click Add to add more files to the archive.

WinZip creates a compressed copy of the selected files in the archive. Therefore you end up with two copies of the file: the original, uncompressed version, still in its original folder, and a zipped one, in the archive. If you wish to send this archive via the Internet, keep both copies. If the purpose of the compression was to save some space on your hard disk, you should now delete the original file and keep only the compressed one (which, in some cases, can be ten times smaller than the original). To delete a selected file automatically, use the Move option in the Add dialog box.

Extracting files

WinZip classic/Actions/Extract

Click to open an archive.

WinZip (Unregistered)

File Actions Options Help

New Open Favorites Add Extract View CheckOut Wizard

Name	Modified	Size	Ratio	Packed	Path

Choose "New" to create or "Open" to open an archive

Click to display its contents.

Open Archive

Look in: Archives

Multimedia_StoryBoard.zip

Select the archive.

File name: Multimedia_StoryBoard.zip

Files of type: Zip files

Open

Cancel

Help

You can compress any file with WinZip: text, images, sounds, etc. However, the compression rate differs depending on the nature of the file (a sound file, for example, may be compressed by as little as 2%, which is insignificant). WinZip is the most common compression program, and zipped files can be uncompressed by most PC users. However, other specialised compression methods are also available such as MPEG for video, for example.

Checklist

1. In the WinZip window, click *Open* to open the archive containing the file you want to extract. It is usually better to copy the archive to a hard disk before opening it.

2. Select the archive you want to open by clicking its name.

3. Click *Open* to confirm. WinZip closes this window and displays the contents of the selected archive.

4. Select the files you want to extract. You can select several files and extract them in one step (see the preceding pages).

⑤ Click *Extract* (extracting a file really means creating an uncompressed copy of it out of the archive). This command then opens another dialogue box.

⑥ Select the folder in which the decompressed files must be saved. You can enter the path directly, or click on a folder in the right pane in the right part of the window.

⑦ Select the files you want to extract: the selected files only, all the files or the files with a name that corresponds to the string you have typed in the *Files* text box.

⑧ Click *Extract* to launch the decompression.

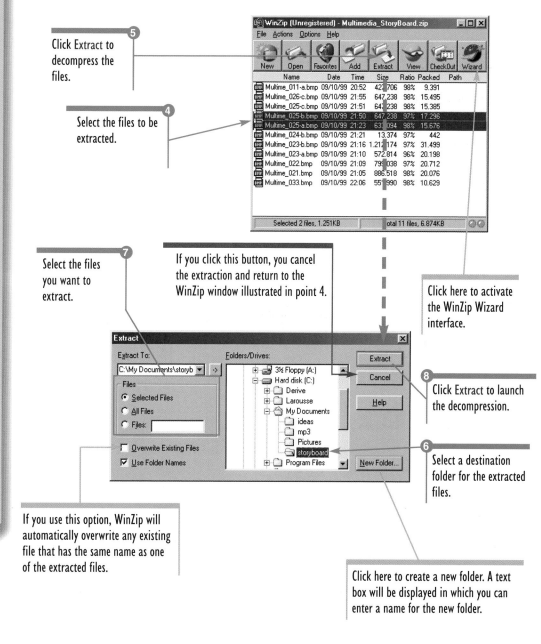

⑤ Click Extract to decompress the files.

④ Select the files to be extracted.

⑦ Select the files you want to extract.

If you click this button, you cancel the extraction and return to the WinZip window illustrated in point 4.

Click here to activate the WinZip Wizard interface.

⑧ Click Extract to launch the decompression.

⑥ Select a destination folder for the extracted files.

If you use this option, WinZip will automatically overwrite any existing file that has the same name as one of the extracted files.

Click here to create a new folder. A text box will be displayed in which you can enter a name for the new folder.

Extracting files using the Wizard interface

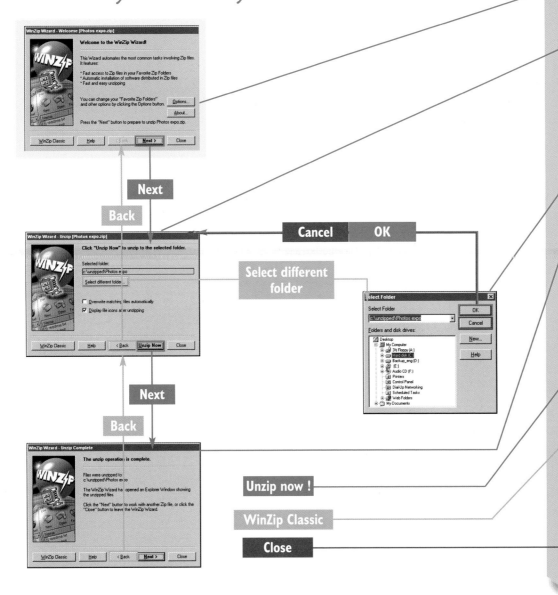

Next

Back

Cancel   **OK**

Select different folder

Next

Back

Unzip now !

WinZip Classic

Close

WinZip Wizard banner screen.

Folder selection dialogue – see notes.
Used to select the folder in which the files will be extracted. The complete path is displayed under 'Selected folder.'

This dialogue box allows you to select a different folder.

The progress bar is displayed, and then WinZip confirms that the extraction has been successfully completed. Click *Next* to extract other files or *Close* to exit WinZip.

Launches the extraction of the selected files.

Used to go back to the WinZip Classic interface.

Closes WinZip.

QuickTime
Start/Programs/QuickTime for Windows

Imported from the Macintosh environment, QuickTime has evolved from a multimedia player to a complete multimedia manager. When you install QuickTime, you install two viewers. MoviePlayer 32-bit is used to view video files in **MPEG** format or in QuickTime format (**.MOV** extension). Picture Viewer 32-bit opens files in **JPG** and **PIC** formats (PIC files usually come from the Macintosh environment). These viewers replicate the Windows multimedia tools, but they also read some special file formats.

When you install QuickTime, a QuickTime icon appears in the control panel. From this icon, you can manage the most important multimedia objects: audio, video, and **MIDI**. These very complete dialogue boxes give a much better overview of the computer multimedia potential than the corresponding Windows managers. You can change the default sampling frequency, for example, as well as check the drivers in use.

QuickTime 32

TIP
QuickTime can be downloaded from the Internet. Search on Yahoo.com to find one for your platform.

HOW TO

To change the sampling frequency:

In the Control Panel, click the QuickTime icon. A dialogue box opens. Click the More button to have access to all tabs. Select the Audio tab. In the Sample Rate, select a frequency of 44 100 Hz (CD quality). Click Apply to apply the change.

QuickTime Control Panel

Setup | Video | **Audio** | MIDI | Files | Components

Device:
AWE64 Wave Out [220] driver version 4.36

Extended Support:
Supports volume control
Supports left and right volume control

Supported Formats:
Mono 8 bit 11.025 kHz
Mono 8 bit 22.050 kHz
Mono 8 bit 44.100 kHz
Mono 16 bit 11.025 kHz
Mono 16 bit 22.050 kHz

Sample Rate
Requested hz: 44100
Actual hz: 44100
☐ Automatic Rate Adjustment

Sample Depth
◉ 16 bit
○ 8 bit

Channels
◉ Stereo
○ Mono

Volume
◉ Audio Driver
○ QuickTime

Close | Apply | Less | Help

Opening files automatically
Windows Explorer/View/Folder Options

As you use Windows Explorer, you will come across numerous files you want to open. There are two basic ways to do this. Either you open the appropriate program and use the File/Open command, then you locate the file and open it. Or you can double-click the name of the file in Explorer. Windows then calls the appropriate application and instructs it to open the file. In order to do this, Windows relies on a program manager, in which different file types are linked to programs that can handle them. This list can be modified easily.

This can be useful for two reasons. First, some file formats may not be associated with programs. They are not common, but it is worth knowing how to create a link when needed. The second reason is that some links, created automatically by Windows, may not be the most appropriate. An image in JPEG format, for example, could be opened by a Web browser (such as Microsoft Internet Explorer, if it is installed on the PC). This is acceptable because JPEG is the most common image format on the Internet. However, a browser will only let you view an image. If you wish to edit it, you need to use an image editing program. Therefore, it may be necessary to cancel the link between the JPEG format and your browser and to create another, pointing to the appropriate software.

HOW TO

In the 'Folder Options' window, click the File Types tab to display the list of recognised file formats, and check the program launched when a file of the type selected is opened. For the example, PSD images (Photoshop) are opened with Photoshop.

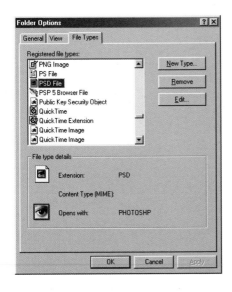

Checklist

Let us suppose that you do not want to open JPEG images with Internet Explorer, but with Paint Shop Pro.

1. Select the 'JPEG Image' type. The program indicates this file type is normally opened with Internet Explorer.

2. Click *Edit* to change the link.

3. Click *Edit* again. The options proposed in this dialog box are not important at this stage.

4. The heading *Application used to perform actions* displays the access path for the linked program. Click *Browse* to be able to open another program.

Change program opened by default

Windows Explorer/View/Folder Options

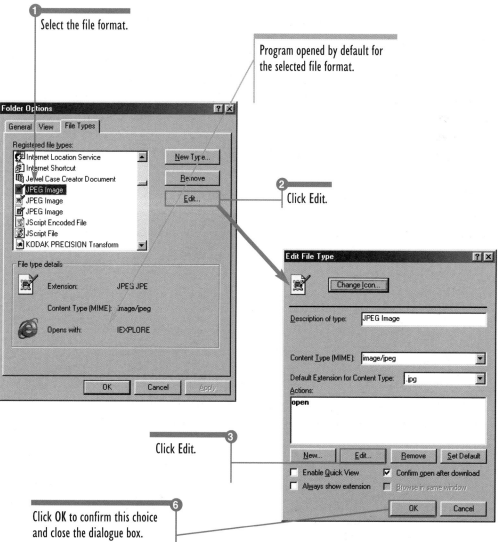

1 Select the file format.

Program opened by default for the selected file format.

2 Click Edit.

3 Click Edit.

6 Click OK to confirm this choice and close the dialogue box.

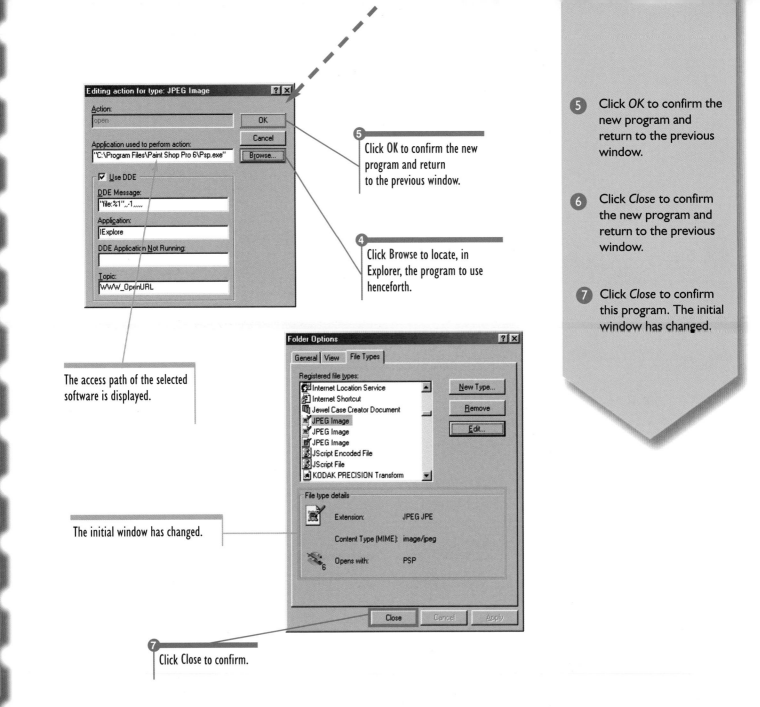

Click OK to confirm the new program and return to the previous window.

Click Browse to locate, in Explorer, the program to use henceforth.

The access path of the selected software is displayed.

The initial window has changed.

Click Close to confirm.

⑤ Click *OK* to confirm the new program and return to the previous window.

⑥ Click *Close* to confirm the new program and return to the previous window.

⑦ Click *Close* to confirm this program. The initial window has changed.

Index

D

INDEX

189

W